THE FOOD CONNECTION

THE
FOOD
CONNECTION

THE BBC GUIDE TO HEALTHY EATING

COLIN TUDGE

BRITISH BROADCASTING CORPORATION

The BBC Food and Health Campaign

This campaign was launched by BBC Education in Autumn 1985 to give information and practical advice on the established links between diet and health.

TELEVISION SERIES

O'Donnell Investigates: The Food Connection, produced by David Cordingley. Part 1 first transmitted on BBC 1 and 2 from September 1985; Part 2 first transmitted on BBC 2 from February 1986.

The Taste of Health, produced by Jenny Rogers. First transmitted on BBC 2 from September 1985.

You Are What You Eat, produced by Anna Jackson. First transmitted on BBC 1 from January 1986.

RADIO SERIES

Not Another Diet Programme, produced by Sarah Rowlands. First transmitted on Radio 4 early 1986.

BBC PUBLICATIONS

The Food Connection: The BBC Guide to Healthy Eating by Colin Tudge

The Taste of Health: The BBC Guide to Healthy Cooking edited by Jenny Rogers

The Campaign was devised by David Cordingley, BBC Continuing Education Television Department

Cover photograph by James Jackson
Diagrams by David Eaton
The diagram on page 100 is reproduced by kind permission of Martin Dunitz Ltd, from 'Don't Forget Fibre in your Diet' written by Denis Burkitt

Published to accompany a series of programmes prepared in consultation with the BBC Continuing Education Advisory Council

ISBN 0 563 21121 0 (paperback)
ISBN 0 563 21205 5 (hardback)

Typeset in 11/13pt Linotron Baskerville by
Rowland Phototypesetting Ltd, Bury St Edmunds, Suffolk.
Text printing by Jolly and Barber Ltd, Rugby, England.
Cover origination by Bridge Graphics, Hull.
Cover printing and binding by Chorley and Pickersgill,
Leeds, England.

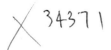

CONTENTS

Foreword   7

1 The principles of good eating I: Consensus   9

2 The principles of good eating II: What is a natural diet?   17

3 Why suppose our diet is at fault?   32

4 Everything you ever wanted to know about fat   39

5 What's wrong with fat?   48

6 Carbohydrate revisited   80

7 The mythology of protein   109

8 Vitamins and minerals   117

9 Salt under pressure   123

10 The sense of staying slim   133

How it affects you: some guide lines on individual consumption
by Maggie Sanderson, Community Dietitian, City and Hackney Health Authority

The Nacne Report   15

What can we do about fat?   72

How much sugar are you eating?   89

How much fibre are you eating?   106

Quick guide to a good diet   147

FOREWORD

There has recently been a remarkable upsurge in interest in food and health in Britain with a plethora of reports over the last few years from the Royal College of Physicians and the Department of Health. As the public comes to learn that our diet in the long term affects our health there will be an ever increasing demand for information presented in a way that can be readily understood.

I am delighted to see this new publication which sets out Colin Tudge's view of the food that we eat, why we eat it and what it does to us once it is absorbed. He brings out very neatly the problems which anybody working in nutrition has in producing a clear-cut message that is guaranteed to be relevant to every individual. The wide-ranging views have been blended into an interesting story which contrasts starkly with the terse style of official reports which are so hard to interpret. These reports reflect the way in which nutritional scientists, struggling with a vast body of literature and so many unknowns, often end up by making formal statements so short that most, if not all, of their colleagues in the field can agree with the official text. I would guess that if this book were sent to thirty or forty nutritional scientists in Britain they would spend three to five years going through it, phrase by phrase, questioning the exact balance of evidence used and finally coming up with a dull consensus document which few general readers would bother to keep on their bookshelves.

I particularly welcome the individual approach Colin Tudge shows in this book and the way in which he makes it clear that absolute proof about the good or ill effects of particular nutritional components can at times be extremely difficult to obtain. For example, the unravelling of the complex details of fat metabolism in the body and the way in which this affects our health could well become an intriguing saga over the next ten years and may never be fully explained. Colin Tudge has produced a remarkably well balanced book with sensible statements and an astonishing range of illuminating examples; I am sure it will be of great help to the general reader who currently feels confused about what the food we eat really does to us. I commend it and hope that it will help to educate us all.

Professor Philip James M.D., Rowett Research Institute, Aberdeen

Chapter 1

THE PRINCIPLES OF GOOD EATING I: CONSENSUS

The question is simple enough: what should human beings eat? Plenty of people are anxious to answer it: doctors, nutritionists, dieticians, chefs, and a host of miscellaneous laiety. But never in the history of human endeavour have so many expert opinions contributed in so short a time to so much confusion as now exists in the field of human nutrition.

We have been told this past 20 years to eat protein – as much as possible. But we have also been told that this is not necessary, for there are people who subsist virtually on roots alone, which hardly contain any at all. We have been told, indeed, that excess protein is undesirable.

We have been told to cut out fat; though at other times, by other experts, that fat doesn't matter, or that it does, but that some fats are much more harmful than others, and some are even beneficial.

We have been told that sugar is the biggest single destroyer of Western civilisation. But we are also told, through television, twice nightly on bad nights, that the very same substance masquerading as 'energy' is what your children need to keep them snug as they snail their way to school, and what you need to carry you through the hypothetical hour of feebleness between lunch and dinner.

We have been told that dietary fibre is just 'roughage' and of interest only to those fixated with their bowels, but told too that it is a panacea, the single solution to the world's food problems.

We have been told that chronic deficiency of vitamins lays us open not only to infection (notably the common cold) but to cancers, and to a whole spectrum of ills from minor lesions of the lip to spina bifida; but told, too, by officially convened committees, that talk of vitamin deficiency in affluent societies is greatly exaggerated.

We have been told that the key to much disorder lies in minerals, some (like sodium) having fairly direct effects on obvious and important properties, such as blood pressure, and some (like magnesium and zinc) having a more devious, but nonetheless significant influence on heart function and fetal growth. But we have also been told that such ideas are far from proven and, in general, are the currency of cranks.

And that is only from the experts. Apart from this, overlaying all this quasi-official instruction, are the voices of vested interests, of genuine cranks, and of groups with particular ideals – vegetarians, for example. Apart from disputes about the proper intake of protein, or the appropriate composition of fat, there are debates of a more metaphysical kind; about, for instance, the difference between 'natural' and 'unnatural', and whether the difference matters. Among the disputants, too, are some whose job it is to obfuscate in order to sell particular products of dubious nutritional value.

The task of this book is to cut a path through the confusion: to look at the modern ideas in nutrition, and to look, as far as space permits, at some of the thinking behind those ideas. We will not tell you what to do (God knows, there has been no shortage of instruction), but help you to appraise the evidence for yourself.

Out of confusion, consensus is born

With such a mass of conflicting ideas and interests, the task we have set ourselves may seem impossible. If one expert says one thing, and another, equally qualified and equally confident, says the precise opposite, how can anyone decide who is right? And as advertisements are bound by the Advertising Standards Authority to declare only what is true and honest, how can we even reasonably dispute what they say?

Yet the position is far from hopeless. In recent years, from several different directions, there are signs of consensus emerging. That in itself is not entirely persuasive since experts have a marvellous propensity for rallying to the wrong flag, but the modern consensus nonetheless has several encouraging features. The first is that it addresses all the components of food: protein, fat, carbohydrates, minerals and vitamins. What is now presented is not a formula that concentrates upon one feature of diet and allows the rest to take care of itself, but one that acknowledges that the human diet is woven from many different threads.

The second is that the modern consensus is internally consistent. Nutritionists in the past have recommended that we should eat more of 'this' (meat, fish and eggs, say, in the great days of protein) and more of 'that' (vegetables, beans and wholemeal bread, for example) and thus effectively told us to eat more of everything (but not too much, mind). The modern consensus instead offers a balance. Whatever is taken away from one portion of the diet, is made up in another.

The third encouraging feature is that the modern consensus is compounded of many kinds of evidence. We will discuss this issue later:

if ever one is to begin to judge who is presenting a plausible argument and who is flying a kite, then it is essential to have some grasp of the nature of scientific evidence. Suffice to say here that in science there really is no such thing as absolute proof: there are merely ideas that stand up to various kinds of test. In addition, when we're exploring the lives of human beings, all our tests are liable to be circumspect, or indirect. To test the effects of particular diets on particular human beings we would have to carry out controlled studies over entire lifetimes, and that cannot be done. So the evidence that has been fed in to produce the modern consensus is compounded of large studies of human beings leading their own lives, of studies of sick people, and of studies of animals and test-tube biochemistry. The evidence thus is inferential, it is in many areas inadequate, it does not all lead in the same direction and it is held together in the end by informed speculation. But there's enough pointing in the same direction – and the informed speculation is tight enough – to add up to a convincing scenario. We are a long way from a definitive thesis on human nutrition. But we do have the makings of an interim statement.

The final encouraging aspect of the modern consensus is that it looks like good biology. Human beings are, after all, animals. The likelihood is that we evolved, as every other animal did, in a state of nature; and survived because we were well adapted to the succession of environments that our ancestors confronted. Some of the wilder and more narrowly based nutritional theories have begged the question: what kind of animal is it that could possibly have evolved to eat the diet that is being proposed? But the modern consensus makes entirely believable suppositions about the kind of animal the human being really is.

We will return to this point shortly. Biological arguments of a philosophical kind have often been used to support or attack particular nutritional scenarios, and for this reason alone it is important to look at what is known about human beings in a state of nature, at least as a contribution to understanding ourselves.

Finally, one of the most encouraging features of the modern synthesis of nutritional ideas is that it is practical. It asks us to do nothing cranky and certainly nothing intolerable. Indeed, modern nutritional ideas are compatible with the finest traditional cuisines. For the first time nutritionists are inviting us, albeit with a few significant caveats, to do what comes naturally.

This point too will be discussed at greater length; indeed, it is one of the principal themes of this book. But first we should look briefly (there is time for detail later) at the consensus itself.

An outline of the new ideas

In summary, the ideas of the modern consensus can be boiled down to a few simple directives. I will take the points component by component.

With *protein* the modern advice, taken all in all, is virtually to let it take care of itself. That is, if you pay proper attention to the major sources of energy in your diet – that is, to fat and carbohydrate – then it is extremely difficult to see how you could be specifically short of protein. This is in sharp contrast to the advice of two decades ago when you would have been invited to pile your plate high, preferably three times a day, with flesh – and then to let the rest of the diet take care of itself. The change of emphasis, and the reasons for it, are discussed more fully on pages 109 to 116.

With *fat*, the advice is more complicated: but the general idea is to eat less of it, and as far as possible to move from a diet rich in animal fats and in vegetable fats of an unspecified nature, to one featuring the polyunsaturated oils of sunflower, safflower, or maize. Fish oil, too, is desirable: that also tends to be polyunsaturated. Deeper discussion is on pages 39 to 79.

Carbohydrate has become the key to the modern diet. If you eat less fat, and if you do not pile your plate with meat, then you would be very short of energy if you did not eat more carbohydrate to compensate. After all, protein, fat and carbohydrate are the only sources of food energy.

It is here that the modern advice differs most conspicuously from that put forward earlier this century, at least until the 1970s. In virtually all previous diets carbohydrates were to be avoided: even bread, the staff of life, has often been publicly deplored. But the crucial distinction today is between unrefined carbohydrate and refined. Carbohydrate, in general, means sugar, starch, cellulose and related compounds from plants, and glycogen from animals. The greatest sources of carbohydrate are the plants. But plant material in a state of nature – unrefined, that is – contains huge amounts of cellulose and other comparable materials, which are the substance of its cell walls and its means of support. It is these cell walls that constitute dietary fibre.

In general, if you eat carbohydrate in unrefined form – complete with dietary fibre – then you should do yourself no harm. Yet the advice is not simply negative: rather, the consensus says, it is in general a good thing to obtain as much of your daily energy as possible from unrefined carbohydrate (that is, from plant material with its fibre still intact). Furthermore, the cheapest, most plentiful and most obvious sources of unrefined carbohydrate are the staples: cereals, pulses and potatoes (and, in tropical countries, roots such as cassava). Cereals and pulses are seeds. Potatoes are tubers and stand in for seeds, since both serve as food stores for the embryo plant, and both, accordingly, contain not only carbohydrate, but a tolerable quota of protein.

All this explains the maxim that if you get the fat right (that is, do not eat much of it) and get the carbohydrate right (that is, eat unrefined carbohydrate in the form of staples), then you should also get the protein right. By eating the best sources of unrefined carbohydrate and little fat or refined carbohydrate, you will also take in a reasonable measure of protein.

Refined carbohydrate, on the other hand, means sugar and starch. Starchy foods are not the greatest evil: the staples, after all, are all rich in starch and we have just discussed their merits. Also, starch (with only minor exceptions) is not generally eaten in pure, extracted form. But sugar, whatever its other ills (and it has several) is a potent source of calories and confers no other nutritional benefits; in other words, in refined form, which is its usual form, it does not come accompanied by other nutrients. Therefore the more you eat refined carbohydrate – that is, the more you eat sugar – the more you will throw your diet, and hence your metabolism, out of balance. The carbohydrate story is discussed in detail on pages 80 to 108.

As for micronutrients, the *vitamins* and *minerals*, we are now very properly offered a number of commonsensical comments, and one serious negative.

The commonsensical comments boil down to the observation that to be complacent about minerals and vitamins is foolhardy. There are very few unequivocal examples of vitamin deficiency diseases in western countries but there is a great deal of anecdotal, circumstantial and occasionally solid evidence to suggest (a) that subclinical vitamin deficiencies could be important; (b) that immigrant children in particular, whose traditional diets have been compromised and not adequately replaced by a western diet, may well show clinical signs of vitamin deficiency, and (c) that some very serious disorders, notably spina bifida, could also, some of the time, result from vitamin deficiency.

In general, the advice boils down to the rather simple observation that you should strive to eat as varied a diet as possible: one rich in vegetables and staples, and eked out with small amounts of meat and fish. I will discuss this further in the next chapter.

The one serious negative concerns salt, alias sodium chloride. A great deal of circumstantial evidence suggests that a diet high in salt predisposes to high blood pressure (hypertension), and high blood pressure predisposing both to heart disease and stroke can be very serious indeed. Furthermore, a high-salt diet does not mean one compounded exclusively of kippers: it means the normal, average, day-to-day diet of the normal, average person. Most of us, as a matter of course, eat at least 10 times and probably nearer 100 times more salt than we actually need.

The advice, then, is to find other ways of flavouring food: and to seek out those few food processors who take the salt story seriously enough to provide low-salt foods.

The salt story, and other minerals, are discussed on pages 123 to 132.

This simple set of recommendations – a diet modest in protein, low in fat, high in unrefined carbohydrate but low in sugar, low in salt but as varied as possible – is the essence of the modern consensus.

It implies (as we shall see) a considerable shift of emphasis from the present western diet, which is high in fat, sugar and salt, and low in unrefined carbohydrate.

But it implies no hardship. In practice we are talking of a diet high in staples, high in vegetables and fruit, and highly spiced if you like, with meat and fish taken in moderate amounts for their flavour. This is not prison fare. This has been the raw material of the world's highest culinary achievements.

Before we move on to detailed discussion of the consensus, I would like to return in the next chapter to the deep question of plausibility. Is the diet as now recommended compatible with what we know of the evolution and biology of human beings? Does it meet the needs of the kind of animals we are?

THE NACNE REPORT

The report is named after the committee that commissioned it, the National Advisory Committee on Nutrition Education. This body was constituted in 1979 and included representatives of the Department of Health and Social Security, the Ministry of Agriculture, Fisheries and Food, the British Nutrition Foundation, Health Education Council and members of the academic community. Its role was to look at means of providing simple and accurate information on nutrition. However, it soon became apparent that it was difficult for the committee to proceed without first defining what constituted a healthy diet. It was therefore decided to ask the Vice Chairman, Professor James, to form a working group, whose task would be to examine the various nutritional issues and make recommendations. This group's deliberations and recommendations have become known as the NACNE report.

In formulating its conclusions the group used as its main sources of information the reports of expert committees, primarily UK based, which had been published in the previous few years. Of the eight main sources, four were DHSS reports, three were produced by the Royal College of Physicians and the eighth report was published by the World Health Organisation. There was therefore nothing new or revolutionary in the NACNE report, but by bringing together expert views on different aspects of nutrition it was able to give an overall view of the subject.

This first problem tackled was that of the balanced diet. What did this mean? The concept of a balanced diet grew out of the view that if a large enough variety of foods was consumed this would prevent deficiencies of any nutrients. In modern Britain, however, deficiencies are no longer the major cause of nutritional disease; other diseases have developed despite the balancing concept in nutrition education. It was felt that the introduction of a greater variety of foods was unlikely to help alter the present disease pattern. Instead, a change in the proportion of food items consumed was needed.

The group then gave quantitative guidelines for the groups of foods that it felt played an important role in the formation of a healthy diet. In the past, advice had been to 'reduce' or 'increase' certain commodities, but no indication was given as to by how much they should rise or fall. By giving quantitative guidelines the working group hoped to provide a reference point to which all parties involved in the production of food and those involved in providing nutritional information and advice to the public could work towards.

The main long-term recommendations are:

1 Fat intakes should be reduced by 25% to provide not more than 30% of the total energy intake. Saturated fatty acid intake should be on average not more than 10% of the total energy intake.

2 Average sucrose intake should be reduced by approximately 50% to 20kg per head per year. Of this not more than 10kg should be derived from snack foods.

3 Fibre intake should be increased by 33% to 30g per head per day. The increase should come mainly from a greater consumption of wholegrain cereal.

4 Salt should be reduced by approximately 25% to 9g per head per day.

5 No recommendations either to increase or decrease total protein intake have been made. Other recommendations would however ensure a greater proportion being consumed from vegetable sources.

6 The energy content of the diet should be sufficient for individuals to maintain optimum body weight and allow adequate exercise.

Since the NACNE report the DHSS have published a report from their own expert committee, COMA (Committee on Medical Aspects/Food Policy). This report has confined itself to the relationship between diet and cardiovascular disease. It makes no specific recommendations on the fibre and sugar content of our diet, but does give quantitative recommendations concerning fat. These are that our total fat intake should be reduced so that it provides not more than 35% of our total energy (or calorie) intake. In addition it states that not more than 15% of this energy should be derived from saturated and trans-fatty acids. (Trans-fatty acids are unsaturated fatty acids which have been changed chemically by food processing. They act in the body in the same way as saturated fatty acids.)

At first sight these fat recommendations appear to be far less restrictive than the NACNE ones, but in fact the two are very similar. In the NACNE recommendations, alcohol is included when assessing the total energy intake of the average person, so the *percentage* total energy derived from fat is lower. When alcohol is removed from the calculations, and the trans-fatty acids added to the figure for saturated fat, the recommendations are almost identical to those made in the COMA 1984 report.

Chapter 2

THE PRINCIPLES OF GOOD EATING II: WHAT IS A NATURAL DIET?

In all advice to human beings there run two contradictory strands. The first says that we must be true to our nature, and that the fundamental task, now that we have buried our natural condition beneath so many artefacts, is to re-discover what that nature is. The second says that it is the proper task of human beings to improve on nature. What nature offers is just raw material for human artistry.

The duologue runs through all human affairs. Thus there are moralists who argue that what is natural is right, even if it seems natural to kill or to exploit; and others who say that if such acts are truly natural, then nature must be contravened. There are aesthetes of the romantic variety, who seek to be buffeted by nature as raw as possible; and others who cannot bear a landscape that has not been shaped by human hand – by Brown, or Repton, or whoever at the time is fashionable.

What is signal to our discussion is that this same duologue runs through medicine and through the discipline of nutrition, which in effect is a branch of medicine; and since the function of this book is not simply to look at current advice but to look at the thinking behind the advice, we should be aware of these subliminal currents.

Thus there have always been doctors who believe that the secret of good health is simply to be 'in tune' with nature: I know of one modern physician, properly qualified and well loved by his patients, who is very reluctant to vaccinate almost anybody for almost anything. Others, as we all know, have in their time sought simply to impose their 'scientifically' proven technique, whether it took the form of a handful of pills, or the latest approved method of giving birth.

In nutrition there have been those who argue that it is sensible and proper to base nutritional ideas upon what is known of human biology and evolution; and those who believe, deep down, that whatever happened in evolution is by definition past, and therefore irrelevant.

It is foolish, in this discussion, simply to take sides. The nature-knows-best argument is sometimes fair enough, and sometimes not. To base morality on what is perceived to be natural seems not only absurd, but deeply pernicious. To destroy natural landscape simply to conform to the fashion of the day can seem somewhat blasphemous. To treat patients simply as case histories is – well, bad medicine.

On the other hand, every conservationist knows that nature that is not managed is soon impoverished; and every doctor knows that nature is far from benign, and that the natural state of human beings is a short and brutish life, plagued by parasites. Some degree of refinement of the natural condition is clearly called for.

What does seem clear, in this as in all human matters, is that extreme positions are usually wrong. More to the point, it is also clear from the empirical history of medicine and of nutritional practice that nature should not be mocked.

We can argue this point specifically, or we can argue it from particulars. In nutrition, the history of the 20th century is peppered with bright ideas that went astray and in the end proved highly pernicious. What those ideas tend to have in common is that they all took a far too simplistic view of the overall biology of human beings. They all assumed that, for practical purposes, human beings could be thought of not as whole animals, but as specific machines with one specific mode of functioning. They all, in short, betrayed contempt for nature; they all sought to improve on nature without truly taking account of what was natural. Three examples will suffice.

First, we may take baby food: infant formulas. Human milk, in some ways, is rather feeble stuff. Compared with the milk of cows, for instance, it is low in protein (and compared with that of seals it hardly qualifies as nutriment at all, though that point has never seriously been used in argument). After the Second World War (as I will explain more fully on page 110) protein was acknowledged as the single most important component of food: get that right, and all else would follow. In addition, the war-time health authorities, given power, had significantly improved the nation's health, so authority, it seemed, knew best. The fashion, therefore, was not for breast milk, but for cow's milk, or at least for infant formula that conformed in content to that of cows.

Among the many shortcomings of the fashion for bottle feeding were the appearance of immune responses, in babies, to formulas based on cow's milk; the overfeeding of many babies in western countries (and their starvation in some Third World countries when the formulas proved too dear); infection in Third World countries, where sterilisation was a problem; obesity in mothers, who failed to dispose of the 30,000 kcal they would normally lose in lactation; and psychological losses, which some psychologists say resulted from a lack of the bonding normally established by breast feeding.

The point of this is not to say that bottle feeding has no place, which would be both dangerous and inaccurate, or that breast feeding is a panacea, because it, too, can raise many problems. It does, however, demonstrate without equivocation the sin of medical hubris: the belief that the pursuit of some simple idea (including, in this case, the idea that protein was the key to healthy development) should be allowed to override what nature had provided. Human milk, by the standards of cows (and seals) is feeble stuff; but it is beautifully adjusted to the needs of human babies.

Sugar provides a second example. Sugar is now recognised as a major contributor to obesity and is undoubtedly the principle begetter of dental caries. But it was not always so. In my memory it has been advertised widely as a 'pure' source of energy. Any suggestion that large amounts of such highly concentrated material could do you harm was dismissed as simple romanticism.

Again, the point is not simply that the advocacy for sugar was misguided, but that it was arrogant. Human beings obviously needed energy. Sugar was a good source of energy, and 'refined' sugar was self-evidently superior to sugar left inside its native plants, diluted by fibre and water. Again, the deep-lying assumption was that human beings could be regarded, for practical purposes, simply as machines, which carried out specific machine-like functions; and any consideration that detracted from that vision was seen to be muddle-headed. Again, the folly of such arrogance has now been revealed.

The third example is that of dietary fibre itself. We will deal with this in proper detail on pages 93 to 108, but it is in this area, perhaps, that the simple mechanistic arrogance of much nutritional theory has been most obvious, and most cruelly exposed. Through much of this century and the last, the food industry has devoted considerable energy to eliminating the fibre from plant food: extracting sugar from grass (cane) and roots (beet), and removing as much as possible of the bran from flour. Those who suggested that the fibre (which until recently was universally known as 'roughage') might actually serve some function tended, in general, to be derided. As late as the mid 1970s an eminent professor of nutrition solemnly advised me that there was 'no evidence' that fibre served any physiological function, except perhaps to relieve constipation, and that there could be no reasonable suggestion that it could possibly protect against serious ailments.

Again, the point is not simply that the expertise that prevailed until recently was mistaken, but that it was arrogant. More, it was arrogant in the very specific sense, that it was an over-simplication of nature. The roots of nutritional science have traditionally been in chemistry, and it was (and is) difficult to analyse the effects of dietary fibre in purely chemical terms. Yet many nutritionists (most, until recently) could not bring themselves to believe that nature might after all be more complicated than they had chosen to believe: so if something could not be explained in chemical terms, then it could not possibly be important.

These three morality tales do not add up to a cast-iron case. Neither are they intended to suggest that everything natural is necessarily good, or that all expertise is bad: both points are sometimes made, and both are nonsense. But they do suggest that in the particular field of human nutrition it pays to be humble. In this instance we should seek to observe nature, as far as possible to understand it, and to work with it. We should not seek to impose grandiose ideas of how nature *ought* to be. Capability Brown may have been able to re-direct a river and flatten a hill in order to create an effect that is better than nature. But if we seek to impose the whims of fashion on our own bodies; if we decide on the basis of our theorising that the body *ought* to appreciate more protein, or should in an ordered world *prefer* to take its energy in the purest possible form, then we are liable to find that nature can rebel. Indeed, we already have clear demonstrations of rebellion.

Besides, the common-sense observation of the biologist is that although we have changed our physical environment decisively in the past 100,000 years, and particularly in the past 10,000 since the development of agriculture, and even more in the 200 since the industrial revolution, we have nonetheless inherited the bodies, and the digestive systems, of human beings who were obliged to live in the wild. It is also self-evident that our ancestors could not have survived in the wild unless they were adapted to it. Of course, we know that they did not survive particularly well: for a million years at least the human being was a fairly rare animal, and until relatively recently few human beings survived their fourth decade. For this, and the more obvious practical reasons, it would not be sensible to suggest that we should all strive to return to a state of nature. But we can seek the ground rules in nature; and we have had enough warnings to see that if nutritionists ever advocate courses of action that deviate too wildly from what might have been possible in nature, then this advocacy is liable to be wrong.

In short, in framing nutritional theories it makes sense to ask what human beings eat when in a state of nature, because the kinds, the proportions and the physical state of things that nature has to offer are the kinds, the proportions and the states of things that shaped our physiology. What, then, is the natural diet of humankind?

Human beings are omnivores

The above statement has the kind of bland simplicity that makes you turn to the next chapter, or indeed give up reading for the day. But it is largely because biologists, and in particular nutritionists, have failed fully to grasp what is implied by being an omnivore that nutritional theories and their corresponding recommendations have so often gone off the rails. They have not had proper respect for the biology of the human animal.

There are many advantages in being an omnivore, if only because there are a great many disadvantages in being anything else. If you are a strict herbivore, for example (that is, a vegetarian), then you have several distinct problems. The first, and main one, is that nutrients in plant food tend to be highly dilute, so to get enough of them you need bulk. Leaves, in particular, may contain 80 per cent water or more; and plant cells, unlike those of animals, are each incarcerated in a thick casing of cellulose and related materials.

Herbivores solve this outstanding problem in one of two ways, or a mixture of the two. Some try to eat only the most concentrated plant foods, such as seeds. The difficulty there, of course, is that seeds tend to be seasonal, especially in temperate climates, so the seed-eaters (such as mice or small birds) veer towards omnivory to make up the difference.

Other herbivores have developed techniques for coping with bulk in general and with cellulose in particular. The ruminant animals such as cows and sheep, for example, have a huge extension of the stomach, known as the rumen, and non-ruminant herbivores such as the horse and elephant have a huge diversion of the hind-gut, known as the caecum. In these chambers the animals mix the chewed vegetation with bacteria, which digest the cellulose and turn it into volatile fatty acids (VFAs) which the cow or horse can then absorb, and which supply these animals with most of their energy.

Though ruminants, horses and elephants are extremely successful animals (which proves that the method works), this technique has obvious disadvantages. Perhaps the main one is that in order to obtain enough food the animal has to eat much of the time, if not most of the time. Another is the sheer mass of food that has to be carried around, internally. And a third, less obvious, one is that the bacteria that so efficiently break down low-grade material, such as cellulose, are extremely wasteful of high-grade material. Thus, though farmers do give high-protein feeds to dairy cattle to improve their milk yield, a large input of protein into a cow is simply a waste: the bacteria 'burn' it all away. Ruminants can not only make do on a low-grade diet; they are *committed* to a low-grade diet, which is why they have to eat all day. Being

a committed carnivore also has its drawbacks, not the least of which is
that prey can be hard to come by (a remarkable number of lion hunts
end in disappointment) and predation can be dangerous for the hunter
as well as the hunted. The food, of course, when they get it, is
remarkably rich, and the carnivore does not need to eat often and
certainly not continuously.

However, Dr Michael Crawford of the Institute of Zoology at the
London Zoo has pointed out that carnivory, in a state of nature, is not all
that it seems. A carnivore that simply ate the muscles of its prey – the
red meat, which in restaurants manifests as the most expensive steak –
would soon suffer severe deficiency diseases, not least through lack of
essential fats. These fats (of which more on pages 43 to 46) are best
represented in offal, notably the liver. The committed carnivore, then,
tends to eat a variety of elements from its prey: offal, red meat and
bones.

Cats are perhaps the most committed carnivores of all. They lack a
particular enzyme that most other animals possess, the function of which
is to manufacture one particular essential fatty acid – an essential fatty
acid found, for all practical purposes, only in meat. This is not to say
that cats need an all-meat diet. They clearly do not. But if they do not
have some meat in their diet, or a diet that specifically takes care of their
special needs for essential fatty acids, then they become severely ill. Not
to put too fine a point on it, their tissues begin to disintegrate.

To be an omnivore, however, gives an animal the best of both worlds.
Plants are there (in the tropics all year round) to provide a steady
background of calories, protein and vitamins: and meat is available now
and again to enrich the diet. Such evidence as there is suggests that this,
in general, is the course that human beings and their primeval ancestors,
have always pursued.

The fossil evidence of human beings is, to say the best of it,
fragmentary. But Africa and Asia in particular have yielded many a
jawbone, thousands of teeth, a sizeable collection of skulls,
miscellaneous legs and arms, and a few almost complete skeletons. This
evidence suggests that human-like creatures originated in Africa three to
four million years ago. Some apparently made destructive tools at an
early stage, and presumably hunted (although the fact that they hunted
says nothing about whether, or to what extent, they also ate vegetation).
Others developed huge jaws and teeth evidently adapted to a diet of
gritty wild fruit.

Much later evidence – from 100,000 years ago – shows the use of fire.
Much later still, 12–10,000 years ago, we find, in the Middle East,
human settlements leading to the beginnings of agriculture. Within

those settlements we find evidence of seeds, evidently gathered for food, and assemblages of animal bones, likewise.

Today a few human societies still live in or close to a state of nature. Some, notably the Eskimos, are very nearly carnivorous: there is very little vegetation, after all, above the Arctic Circle. Some, notably the aborigines of Japan, are virtually vegetarian. Most are hunter gatherers and/or slash/burn cultivators: their diet consists of a background of locally available vegetation, roots, leaves, fruits and seeds, and whatever animal food (from termites and grubs to fish and big game) that they can catch.

Some authors, impressed by the weapons of destruction found with some of the earliest human remains, have argued that human beings are 'naturally' carnivorous; this, so some have argued, is the basis of human aggression. The latter theory seems to me easily disposed of – if you want aggression, go and have an argument with a stallion – but more important is that this thesis has been used, primarily at the height of the protein boom in the 1950s and 1960s, to argue that the 'natural' diet of human beings is one very high in meat, and in which carbohydrate (plant food) was merely a subsidiary to supply the occasional vitamin (notably C).

Others, including some members of the modern vegetarian movement, have sought to demonstrate that human beings are 'naturally' herbivorous. This argument has often been made on anatomical grounds: the fact, for example, that human beings can move their jaws from side to side, which implies a predilection for grinding plant food, and the fact that human beings do have commodious guts, compared with carnivores, which implies an early commitment to a plant diet.

One objection to this particular vegetarian argument is that far less can be inferred about an animal's natural diet by looking at its anatomy, than is often supposed. Giant Pandas, for example, are bears, and therefore members of the Carnivora. Their anatomy is that of a carnivore. Yet the diet, primarily of bamboo shoots, is almost exclusively vegetarian. (They do not, incidentally, employ bacteria to produce energy from the cellulose in bamboo. They simply eat an enormous amount of bamboo – and derive their energy from the sugar it contains.) Wart-hogs, as it happens, are vegetarian; whereas forest hogs, with an almost identical anatomy of teeth and guts, are omnivorous.

But we need not waste too much time with such specifics. The overall point is that if you look at the fossil evidence (sparse though it is); if you examine the somewhat more abundant, early archaeological evidence; and if you look at the people alive today who still live as hunter-gatherers, then there are only two tenable conclusions. The first is that versatility is the name of the game: human beings, and their humanoid ancestors, really can and did adapt to an enormous range of diets. But the second is that specialists, like Eskimos or Japanese aborigines, are the exceptions. The basic human condition is omnivorousness.

But being an omnivore means a great deal more than eating everything in sight. It is worth looking in small detail at what it does imply, for the implications are highly instructive.

Consider, first, the composition of the food eaten by our ancestors and far-flung relatives: its chemistry and physical structure.

Plants, which for most people are the basis of diet, are not only unrefined in a state of nature but are uncultivated. When people bring plants into cultivation they take steps to 'improve' them: they select the individuals with the biggest seeds, the fleshiest fruits or roots, the most succulent leaves. But most of the seeds found in nature are small, which means they have a very high proportion of husk. The fruits, for the most part, are mean, and the leaves and roots are fibrous in the literal sense, with an internal scaffold of wood and string.

Today there is talk of high-fibre diets. But when it comes to fibre, compared to our ancestors, we are in a different league. When the modern nutritionist advocates a high-fibre diet, he means about 30 grams a day. Modern African villagers on their usual diet may have four or five times this; but they are eating cultivated plants, and their intake of fibre is far less than that of hunter-gatherers, for example in New Guinea.

Such huge intakes of fibre are probably far from ideal. No nutritionist I have ever come across advocates an intake of 200 grams a day. But this figure does serve to put our own paltry intake in perspective. The human gut may well be stretched, literally, when confronted with the plant intake of a hunter-gatherer; indeed, such extreme input can actually be dangerous. The fact is, however, that both in the past and in the present the human gut has had to become adapted to enormous intakes of fibre, and still is capable of dealing with it.

However, today's hunter-gatherers, and by inference our ancestors, may eat a huge variety of plants: tens, even hundreds of species. Botswanian huntsmen, when pressed, listed 85 species of edible plant, and 54 animals besides. The modern supermarkets take pride in the variety they offer, and indeed there are hundreds of 'lines'. But most of the items are based on only a few ingredients, of which the greatest is wheat flour. The variety is conferred largely by additives, of which there really are hundreds. This observation is not meant to be cynical, or even particularly bleak, and supermarkets are not all bad. The point, however, is that the variety that modern nutritionists now recommend is very clearly precedented in nature. If a human animal eats a great many different things then it is liable to pick up a fair proportion of the entire spectrum of essential minerals and vitamins. If an animal eats only a few different things (and the modern human diet is low in total number of species), then it is quite likely to be, in some respects, deficient.

The meat eaten by our hunter-gatherer ancestors and relatives would also have differed radically from our modern conception of it. For one thing, it probably would not have been found in enormous abundance; and what with the difficulties of storage, and the dangers of putrescence, it would not have formed the centrepiece of every meal.

But there are more significant differences, again as emphasised by Dr Crawford. Modern meat from domestic animals is fatty. Even when it looks lean, it is marbled with fat, which runs between the muscle fibres: that is what gives it its succulence. The meat of wild animals is lean, and such fat as it contains tends to be structural.

When the protein fad was at its height, some nutritionists were apt to suggest that the reason modern humans are innately fond of meat, or at least seem to be, is that they descended from ancient hunters who pursued meat (the story went) in search of protein. The suggestion was not, of course, that our ancestors consciously sought protein because they liked the taste, but that they were chronically protein-deficient and sought the thing they were deficient in. This, as we will discuss shortly, is something that several species of animal have been shown to do.

However, what seems to me far more likely on common sense grounds is that our distant ancestors were not specifically short of protein, but permanently somewhat low on energy. Their plant food, as we have seen, was highly dilute, and they would have had to have eaten at least six kilograms a day to acquire even a modest 1500 kcal* or so. Their animal food would have been none too common, and the little they had was lean.

So I humbly suggest, as a contribution to original nutritional thinking, that what hunter-gatherers truly feel the lack of is fat. Fat, after all, is the richest of all natural sources of energy, and of all the components of food it is the one that produces the deepest sense of satiety. Wild animals do not have much fat in their muscles but they do have it, as all creatures do, in their brains and in their bone marrow, and it is perhaps no accident that some of the earliest tools of mankind were apparently designed for the bashing of skulls.

* Kilocalories (kcal) are the units in which the energy value of food is traditionally calculated by nutritionists and the food industry.

I am not suggesting, of course, that because our earliest ancestors sought fat, that we should do so too in order to be more natural. The key difference between now and then is that what for us is all too common, for them was a rare treat. The lesson (as we will discuss later) is that if we still regarded fat as a rare and delicate treat today, then it would give us very few problems.

The general point is that a kill to our ancestors was not just a source of red meat or, more specifically, of protein. All of the animal would have been eaten for its flavour, its variety of textures and for the occasional treats of fat. Again, as with primitive plant food, we see an innate predilection for variety. The liver has become a suspect organ today because of its high content of cholesterol; but it is also an admirable source of uncommon vitamins, notably B12, and to people for whom all forms of fat are a luxury, a little dietary cholesterol is of no consequence.

In short we find, if we think sensibly about it and look humbly at the evidence, that our ancestors and our exotic relatives are, in general, adapted to a diet that in broad outline is similar to the modern consensus. It is high in unrefined carbohydrate (rather heavy, if anything, on the fibre) and practically devoid of refined carbohydrate; it is modest in protein; low in fat and almost certainly adequate, if not rich, in most of the minerals and vitamins by virtue of its extreme variety.

There are two snags, however. The first is that being a hunter-gatherer is somewhat limiting. It isn't necessarily easier to be a farmer, but once you have got farming going and are nicely settled with plenty of children, then you are liable, inevitably, to oust the hunter-gatherers. That seems to be the way of the world.

The second is that the patterns of behaviour necessary to a successful, wild omnivore can be deeply pernicious when carried into the more settled world of agriculture and commerce: and even more pernicious when led astray by the sirens of food processing.

So we should learn from our wild ancestors not simply what they ate; but how, perforce, they behaved. And whereas we might reasonably seek to emulate their diet, we should be very chary of their instincts.

This may seem like special pleading, for why should we choose to follow some aspects of our ancestors' lives, yet reject others? The reason is that, physiologically, we are very similar to them, and what was good for them, in principle, should be good for us. But the environment we have created for ourselves is quite different from theirs. They lived constantly with the threat of deprivation, if not of starvation. We live surrounded by plenty. Their instincts were, so it seems, almost entirely acquisitive, and it's this acquisitiveness, which we've inherited, that is the source of our present ills.

We should look then, briefly, at the natural instincts of omnivores. The point here is not to pander to the beast within, but to learn to control its appetites.

The ways of the omnivore

As I have said, there are clear advantages in being an omnivore. This seems obvious even on theoretical grounds, but there are two animals that seem to demonstrate the case. The first is the rat, which is a highly accomplished omnivore and is one of the most ubiquitous of mammals; and the other is the human being, whose diet is even more varied, and who is equally ubiquitous. But there are snags, too. Omnivory is not easy. If you are a giraffe, with a long neck and equally spectacular tongue, then you may simply stick your head up into the acacia trees and browse from morn till night. If you are a lion, you chase whatever moves, unless you can find something that's already dead. But if you are an omnivore, the whole world is potentially edible. Everything that grows, and even a few things that do not (including salt) may, in principle, be nourishment.

Yet the world is full of pitfalls. Many things that can be eaten are simply not nourishing; and if you are a rat, or a human being, living in the wild, you cannot afford to spend too many days chewing at things that in nutritional terms have no substance. Many things, too, object so strongly to being eaten that they produce poisons; or, if they are normally edible, may 'go off', and so become poisonous.

The omnivore must, then, be very good at selection and must select according to two principles. The first is simply to obtain enough of the 40 to 50 different nutrients (including vitamins and different fatty acids) that animals require – and not only to obtain enough, but to achieve a proper balance; and the second is to avoid being poisoned.

Studies of humans and rats have shown that both animals possess a battery of devices to help them to recognise and seek out what is most nourishing, and shun what is not. These devices are arranged as a two-line whip. At the basic, physiological level are a range of *ad hoc* mechanisms and instincts that for the most part keep the animal very well on beam. At the higher level both animals may bring to bear their considerable brain-power.

One of the mechanisms which both rats and humans possess is an arrangement of specific taste receptors for certain foods that are of particular significance – either because they are likely to be nourishing, or likely to be poisonous. Both, for instance, have receptors in the mouth that are triggered exclusively by sugar, salt and bitterness. In the wild, sugar and salt can be rare, but the modest quantities in which they occur are valuable: it pays to be alert to their presence. Bitterness, by contrast, often signifies toxicity.

Both rats and humans also know when they have had enough; they have built-in mechanisms of satiety. These mechanisms are based on a great deal more than simply having a full stomach. It's not unusual to feel bloated and yet unsatisfied. Furthermore, these mechanisms are to some extent specific. Thus you (or a rat) can feel replete of calories ('couldn't eat another thing') but still feel the need for the sweet acidity of fruit; or, you may eat huge piles of fruit and still feel the need for something 'substantial' – which in practice tends to mean fat, the most calorific food of all.

To some extent (so experimental evidence suggests) these specific mechanisms of satiety are geared to the specific mechanisms of taste. There is evidence, for example, that a rat is attracted by the taste of salt when it is deficient in salt; but finds salt less attractive (for example will take fresh water rather than salty) when it is not deficient. That we (and rats) should possess innate mechanisms that drive us to consume particular foods in which we are deficient is remarkable. But there is direct evidence that they exist, and it is hard to see how we could live without them.

Superimposed on these innate mechanisms is the input of the higher reaches of the nervous system: sight, memory, general experiences, mood and attitude. In nature, nourishing foods are not necessarily tagged with sweetness, but may be flavoured in a thousand other ways. Research at the University of Birmingham, England, by David Booth, and by Robert Bolles and his colleagues at the University of Washington, USA, has shown that rats and humans can cope with this too by the mechanism of 'learned satiety'. If a rat is given something very nourishing flavoured with vanilla and something not very nourishing flavoured with aniseed, then after a time it will develop a preference for vanilla. But this preference is not innate, as a preference for sweetness is innate. If the situation is reversed, and the good food is flavoured with aniseed, then it quickly comes to prefer aniseed.

A similar range of mechanisms divert the omnivore away from whatever is toxic. In general, both rats and humans are averse to bitterness: that is the mirror image of the innate predilection for sugar. The higher level mechanisms of aversion are beautifully demonstrated by rats whenever a farmer tries to kill them with poisoned bait. At first, the rat is intensely curious – in nature, the omnivore has to take all potential foodstuff seriously. But it is also intensely suspicious. Its final course of action, typically, is a compromise. It takes a tiny nibble and then leaves the food alone. If it still feels well after 24 hours or so, it will go back for a proper meal. This is why rats can be so difficult to poison: they are equipped by nature to avoid what is poisonous. Successful rat poisons, just to round the point off, tend to be those that kill cumulatively and slowly, without producing symptoms in the short term. Warfarin, for example, kills slowly by internal haemorrage.

We have all experienced the effects of the mechanisms that the rat employs so astutely. We have all of us eaten perfectly pleasant meals and then started to feel ill, possibly for some quite different reason. But afterwards, even if the illness had nothing whatever to do with the food, we have been unable for some time to 'face' whatever it was we had eaten.

At a more general level, both humans and rats are very clearly influenced in their eating by what their peers and elders eat. Experiments on suckling rats have shown that the pups, when weaned, tend to prefer food of the kind eaten by their mothers even if they have never seen such food themselves. Presumably (there is no other explanation) some whiff of the food permeated through to them through the milk. Thus the pups are given a head start. When they go out into the world they already know that there are some flavours they can safely seek; those, indeed, that sustained their mothers.

At the University of Sussex, Astrid Posadas-Andrews and Tim Roper showed that rats could learn to like a novel food that they had never seen before if one of the rats in their colony was taken away and fed on it first. Presumably, when the rat returned to the fold, the others got a sniff of what it had been eating from the remnants on its whiskers. Again, the rats who stayed at home were given a reason to suppress their native suspicion. If another rat can eat the food and get away with it, then it cannot be all bad.

Humans, again, seem to work by much the same principles. It is not coincidence, and nothing whatever to do with genes, that every Italian boy and girl grows up with a penchant for olives and garlic – which the English, until fairly recently, have in general abhorred. The point about national cuisines, indeed, is not simply that they tend to be based on local ingredients, but that each is built around a fairly circumscribed collection of flavours, which gives the cuisine a prevailing character. Elizabeth and Paul Rozin of the University of Pennsylvania have christened such prevailing characters the 'flavour principle'. Thus the flavour principle of Mediterranean cooking tends to be compounded of oil, garlic, tomatoes and herbs. In many parts of India the flavour principle manifests itself in coriander, cumin and turmeric; and so on.

It's clear, too, that social influence can lead people to overcome natural aversions, and even turn those aversions into predilections. Thus every small boy screws up his face at his first sip of his father's beer; but many a small boy then grows up to crave a good pint. Humans in general avoid putrescence, yet learn to love Camembert and pheasant so rotten it falls off its hook. Yet these acquired likes and dislikes remain fairly specific. Lovers of Camembert, for instance, would not necessarily take readily to rancid yak's milk, as favoured in Tibet.

In general, what we observe both in rats and humans is immense curiosity about new foods, tempered by immense caution. In general, these are exactly the qualities an omnivore needs if it is to survive in the wild. It has to be curious, or it would not find sufficient variety, and perhaps not find enough to eat at all. It has to be conservative, or it will quickly be poisoned. It has to remember what it has eaten, and how it felt afterwards: it has only one life, and has to learn quickly, as it goes along. But it should, too, be able to contract the learning process by learning from others: if parents like the food, and peers seem to do well on it, then it is worth suspending caution. But when, as happens after a time, the omnivore has learned a repertoire of likes and dislikes that satisfies its needs, it is no longer necessary to be so curious. Then the animal can reasonably become set in its ways. In humans, the pattern of diet that is firmly fixed upon is given coherence by a prevailing flavour principle.

Demonstrably, these mechanisms work; if not, rats and humans would not flourish as they clearly do. But they have also been shown to work by specific experiments. In the 1930s Curt Richter at Johns Hopkins University in Baltimore, USA, presented rats with a range of foods, to which they could help themselves. The rats chose a balanced diet; and if they were made to be nutritionally deficient, then they deliberately selected the foods they lacked. Clara Davis showed the same principles at work in children in hospital (though she did not experimentally produce nutritional deficiencies). She presented them with a range of about 20 foods – cereals, milk, meat, vegetables and fruit. They too, like the rats, selected what they needed, and grew healthily and normally.

Yet the mechanisms that guide the appetites of rats and human beings are not infallible. They have one fatal flaw. They were designed, by evolution, to enable the rat or the human animal to survive in the wild. The wild is a hard place in two distinct ways. Firstly, it does not gratuitously provide vast quantities of food; or rather, if food is ever abundant, then there will be plenty of competition to get at it. Secondly, nature has no interest whatever in making animals happy. Animals may adapt to what nature makes available – indeed they have to. But nature will not set out to titillate.

In general, then, the appetites of rats and humans are geared to austerity. Though they do have mechanisms which tell them that enough's enough (wild animals do not stuff themselves gratuitously at every opportunity), they are, in general, geared to finding as much as they can. The specific predilections for sugar, or fat, or salt, are intended to help the animal persist in seeking out what is particularly valuable, but in nature is particularly rare. Take away the austerity, pander to the specific appetites, and the feeble mechanisms that say enough's enough can simply be overridden. In today's society three distinct forces are at work to outmanoeuvre the natural constraints on appetite.

The first is that food is simply more available. Meat, in particular, which used to be the other side of a three-day hunt, is now there for the taking. Fat, which once could be obtained in quantity only by bashing in the skull of a fair-sized beast, has become ubiquitous. Sugar, once to be found in concentrated form only when guarded by bees, is now the universal thickener, preservative and flavouring.

The second is that modern food is more concentrated. This point is sometimes obvious (there is nothing in nature that corresponds to a white loaf) and sometimes less so. A chunk of lean and stringy meat from the thigh of some gazelle, for example, is far less calorific than the equivalent muscle from a modern fat lamb.

The third is that, instead of nature casually offering provender to those adapted to it, we have several huge sections of society – farmers, food processors, shop-keepers – urging us to consume; and advertisers, supported by psychologists, assiduously gearing every product to our innate, but inappropriate, instincts. The appetites that evolved to help us to find rare but valuable nutrients, against whatever odds, have been teased into addictions. Our jungle ancestors learned to live with austerity. In our jungle, we must learn to steer a course through abundance.

It's obvious, however, that the modern dietary scene is far from bleak. Human beings in modern affluent societies are bigger, in general, than people in more primitive societies, and live, on average, at least twice as long as, say, hunter-gatherers. Just because diet is very different in composition from that of our ancestors does not mean that it is completely wrong. Indeed, as we do seem in some obvious ways to be better fed than in the past, why should we feel that there is room for improvement?

That will be the main subject of this book. But first we should look in slightly more detail at the food we eat today, so we know what it is that might be changed.

Chapter 3

WHY SUPPOSE OUR DIET IS AT FAULT?

The facts seem simple enough; or if they are not simple, they are at least familiar. Human beings in affluent, western societies on average live twice as long as most people have lived through most of history, and are often remarkably healthy well into old age. On the other hand, they suffer from an unenviable catalogue of diseases, which cause great misery and which cut short many people's lives even when they seem, on the surface, to be in the best of health. Furthermore, many of these diseases are rare or virtually unknown in societies which in all material ways seem to be far less fortunate, and where, in general, people seem far more prone to disease. These diseases – so-called 'diseases of affluence' – include disorders of the gut and its associated systems (constipation, piles, diverticular disease, cancer of the colon, gallstones); diabetes; and disorders of the cardiovascular system, including coronary heart disease and stroke.

For many reasons, not the least of which is common sense, it seems that these diseases of affluence are probably occasioned at least in part by diet. Indeed, as this book relates, there are now some very good ideas on why certain aspects of our diet may be harmful. On the other hand, it's clear that there is very little certainty among the experts. What there is is a great deal of debate, not to say controversy, not to say rancour. How come? As tax-payers we support research which includes nutritional research. So why can't the nutritionists stop passing opinions, and tell us precisely and unequivocally what we are doing wrong, and what we should do to put things right?

The problem would not be difficult (it would be immensely complicated, but not conceptually difficult) if human beings were inexpensive, easily kept laboratory animals, and if scientists were rich (that is, had huge grants to draw on) and lived a very long time. Such an image is distasteful (to scientists as much as to everyone else), but it is also instructive, so we will explore it briefly.

Suppose, for example, that our hypothetical mega-scientist wanted to test the idea that excessive intake of fat leads to coronary heart disease.

The obvious way to go about this would be to keep two colonies of laboratory humans, one fed a high-fat, and the other a low-fat diet. Preliminary observations would reveal that human beings are extremely variable in their response to fat. Therefore, in order to reveal the effects of diet clearly, he would have to have large colonies. After all, the easiest way to see whether coronary heart disease was occurring or not, would be to observe the incidence of heart attacks. But although heart attacks are common, they do not occur in every family or even in every squash club, every week. You would expect to see only a few heart attacks, among a few thousand men, over several years. Therefore, in order to produce statistically significant differences between the high-fat colony and the low-fat colony, the scientist would have to keep thousands of subjects, for many years.

Another possibility, well worth investigating, is that the changes in the arteries that lead to coronary heart disease may begin early in life. Changes occurring in childhood may, theoretically, be as important as developments in middle years. To test this important hypothesis our tireless super-scientist would have to maintain his colonies of several thousand individuals through their entire lives.

Even when the experiment had run its course, and the results were in and showed (let us suppose) that the high-fat colony did indeed suffer more heart attacks, the scientist's joy would be short-lived. His peers would ask for more details. Why, for example, *should* fat cause coronary heart disease? One hypothesis would be that it helps to cause damage to the arteries of the kind known as atheroma. To test this thoroughly, it would be best to develop a genetically uniform strain of subjects, feed them a high-fat diet throughout their lives, and examine (that is, dissect out) their arteries at intervals.

But all this is a bit crude. What about the effects of different kinds of fat? Does polyunsaturated fat have the same effects as saturated? Short-chain the same as long-chain? What of dietary cholesterol? What of the effects of other factors – total calories, protein intake, intake of minerals and vitamins, influence of various forms of carbohydrate, refined and unrefined? What is the influence of non-dietary factors, such as stress? Surely all this requires investigation?

So it does. Back to the drawing board. Instead of two colonies, we should have several dozen, so that we can examine various combinations of factors. We should make the colonies extra large, so that we can examine individuals at intervals to explore their metabolism in detail. After a few centuries (given that the human beings managed to live for 80 years or so, to explore the full effects) there should be a clear answer.

That is the kind of route that would have to be pursued to give the kind of detailed answers, with the appropriate degree of certainty, that ideally are required. And it is of course ludicrous. Human beings cannot be treated as laboratory subjects in that way, and even if they could, the sheer magnitude of the experiments that would need to be done to give crystal clear results would be cripplingly expensive and long-winded. We either throw up our hands in despair, then, or seek varying degrees of compromise.

Modern nutritionists deal, if they deal with people at all, with real people. Those who do work on laboratory animals for the most part use rats as their subjects. Their funds are limited and so is the time-scale: 10 years is a long time in the life of a research project, although it may be a short time in the genesis of some of the affluent world's most destructive diseases. The answers they seek must be cobbled together not from the theoretically ideal experiment done on theoretically ideal subjects over an indefinite period, but from whatever in practice can be observed, under whatever circumstances can be contrived.

Where does the evidence come from?

In practice there are five principal sources of information. Each reflects some aspect of the ideal, but impossible experiment outlined above, but each falls short of the ideal.

The first source of relevant information is from *epidemiology*, the study of disease patterns. The basis of epidemiology is to observe and measure; and having measured, to correlate. Thus it's observed that coronary heart disease occurs mainly in men, mainly in old age but increasingly in the middle years, and in some countries more than in others. The fact that it varies in incidence from society to society suggests that racial and/or environmental factors are involved. The fact that incidence of the disease in any one country does not depend upon the people's race or colour but upon the society they live in, suggests that environmental factors must be more important than racial.

Then it's a question of asking how the societies with a high incidence differ from those with a low incidence, and what those with a high incidence have in common, and what those with a low incidence have in common. It transpires (as is described in Chapter 5) that those with a high incidence, among other things, tend to eat a great deal of fat, and those who have a low incidence eat little fat, and so on.

Comparing the incidence of disease between different societies is known, somewhat unsurprisingly, as a 'between-populations' study. It is at least comforting to be able to supplement such studies with 'within-population' studies. Thus, if we hypothesise that a high-fat intake predisposes to coronary heart disease, then on the face of it it ought to be possible to show that within any one country, people who eat a lot of fat suffer more heart disease than those who do not. Sometimes such within-population studies do bear out hypotheses; but we should not be too disappointed if they do not. No-one would doubt, for example, that the reason people get fat is that they eat more than their body needs to stay slim. To suggest that it would be possible to grow fatter while starving would be to suggest that the human metabolism can defy some of the most fundamental laws of physics. But though it is true that the people of Britain, where obesity is common, tend to eat more in general than the people of Bangladesh, where it is not, (a between-population comparison), it is not true that fat people in Britain consistently eat more than thin people in Britain. The fact seems to be that some people are remarkably good at conserving energy and can grow fat on very little, whereas some people have metabolisms that squander energy, and tend to stay thin whatever they eat. Some scientists get very worried when within-population studies fail to confirm the ideas generated by between-population studies. They should worry less. Any success of within-population studies in this particular field is something of a bonus.

Epidemiological studies have several drawbacks, both practical and theoretical. Among the practical drawbacks is that there may not be enough societies, or enough people within particular societies, to give statistically useful results. Thus, in the whole fat/coronary heart disease story, the fate of Eskimos living on their traditional diet is highly intriguing. They eat a lot of fat, but they do not suffer from coronary heart disease. The reason, apparently, is that the fat they eat is highly polyunsaturated. However, though that seems to be a sound idea, supported by many strands of evidence, it is not one that can be resolved by epidemiology. Among many snags is the fact that there are not enough Eskimos living on a traditional diet to produce *statistically* significant differences between their rate of heart attack and other people's.

In addition, epidemiology can show correlation, but it cannot alone show cause. Societies with a lot of heart disease eat more fat than societies that do not. They also watch more television, spend more time driving cars, and, probably, these days, have more home computers. It is useful to know that fat is correlated with heart disease *if* it actually causes the disease. If it is a cause, then presumably we could reduce heart disease by eating less fat. But if it is not a cause, eating less fat would not be helpful. Following this logic we may reasonably assume that a ban on home computers would not be helpful. Epidemiology is extremely powerful and can certainly help us to home in on factors that demand to be taken seriously. But it cannot alone demonstrate that the factors it identifies are crucial: that is, that the removal of those factors would solve the problems.

Epidemiology is largely passive. Its task is to observe what exists. After epidemiology has alerted us to particular factors we need trials to assess their importance, trials in which we control the action in order to test particular ideas. Such trials may take various forms. Sometimes they take the form of *clinical trials*, where the aim is to try to cure or prevent a disease believed to be associated with a particular factor. Clinical trials have many advantages as sources of information. The subjects are human, which means they are of the right species. In addition, unlike most humans under such circumstances, they are well motivated and often do as asked. Medical professionals remain in control of the trials and produce plenty of sound measurements. The data produced are, or should be, of the kind that qualifies as 'hard'. In addition, the doctor can directly test cause and effect. If he thinks a particular food (such as dietary fibre) might have a particular effect (such as reducing blood cholesterol) then he can give that food and see whether it does or does not.

The trouble with clinical trials is that they tend to deal only with limited numbers of people over limited periods, and the people involved are already ill. One consequence of the latter point is that the information arrived at may be highly suggestive, but may not answer the most important questions. For example, it is now clearly established that patients with diverticular disease benefit if they take a diet high in fibre: their symptoms diminish and the need for surgery is greatly reduced. That is a good solid fact and good solid facts are hard to come by. However, that good solid fact does not tell us whether lack of fibre causes diverticular disease in the first place. We may infer that this is the case, and suggest to people that they ought to eat more fibre to reduce the risk of diverticular disease. But until large numbers of people have eaten large amounts of fibre and developed significantly less diverticular disease than similar people eating less fibre, then we cannot say for certain that lack of fibre is a cause, or that eating more fibre will reduce your chances of falling foul of this particular ailment. The success of clinical trials makes this a strong possibility, but in the absence of an investigation along the lines of our hypothetical ideal experiment, a possibility – inference – is what it remains.

There are also innate ethical problems in all clinical trials. One, much vaunted, is that such suggested new treatments might actually prove harmful. But there is another ethical difficulty which is more subtle and sometimes of much greater significance. This is that no doctor would offer his patients a treatment unless he thought that treatment would be beneficial. But the only way he can definitively test the efficacy of the treatment is by comparing the treated group with *matched controls* – people of a similar age, sex and race, and with a similar complaint, who are not offered the treatment. The problem then arises – is it right to withhold the treatment from the control patients, if that treatment is believed to be beneficial? If it is withheld, patients may suffer who might have been helped. If it is not withheld from some, then it will be impossible to pass final judgement on whether the treatment works or not, and difficult, therefore, to recommend that treatment to the world at large, with the possibility of benefiting many thousands of people. Usually such ethical problems need cause little angst, but sometimes they raise serious dilemmas and in general emphasise the point that there is a limit to the extent to which human disease can be explored through the study of human beings.

Trials can be done, of course, on a preventive basis. These are called *intervention studies*. Groups of people are induced to change their habits and as time goes on it is possible to see whether their incidence of a particular disease goes down. There have indeed been some wonderful, extensive trials along these lines in recent years. Among them was a study in the Finnish province of North Karelia, which in the 1970s had the highest incidence of coronary heart disease in the world. There, the inhabitants of the entire province were encouraged to change their diets (eat more polyunsaturated fat and less saturated) and the most hypertensive were offered treatment to reduce their blood pressure. The incidence of coronary heart disease went down, which seemed to vindicate the notion that high-fat intake and hypertension are not only correlated with their disorder but also helped to cause it.

The only snag here was that the incidence of heart disease also went down in another Finnish province, Kuopio, whose inhabitants were not similarly encouraged. The most likely explanation is that the Kuopians, also worried about their high incidence of heart attack, began spontaneously to follow the lead of the Karelians, but it could be (however unlikely it may seem) that some entirely extraneous factor, unmeasured and untested, affected both populations simultaneously. The Karelian trial is not invalidated: far from it. But it does show that in the real world, the best-laid investigations are bedevilled, not least (and, some would say, to the credit of the human species) by the unpredictability of human behaviour.

Because human beings are so intractable and are universally acknowledged to have 'rights', investigators conduct much of their research on *laboratory animals*. It is not possible to study the effects of controlled diets on large populations of human beings through several generations, but it is possible to perform such studies on rats. It's been demonstrated many many times, and in many different contexts, that such investigations are informative. Medical knowledge rests to an incalculable extent on studies conducted on animals, and no-one who has ever been seriously ill, and rescued by some drug or technique of surgery, can doubt that the knowledge is indeed relevant to human beings. On the other hand, animals of different species do respond differently to food and are different in many metabolic details. The perennial criticism of animal experiments – that animals are not humans – remains perennially valid.

Finally, nutritional scientists have gained many insights by asking their friends or students to take part in trials to test the effects of drinking fizzy pop and subsisting on wholemeal bread or whatever. The advantage of such *human experiments* is that the subjects are generally well motivated (the experimenter might be their professor, for example) and the data should be solid. The disadvantage is that such experiments can run only for a limited time and tend to be conducted primarily on fit, young people who are not usually those most at risk of nutritional disorder.

Well corroborated nutritional theories, then, are not easy to come by. Ideas are simple enough to produce; indeed throughout this century they have been turned out, nineteen to the dozen, by amateur and professional alike. But to test those ideas is never simple. The evidence that can be brought to bear in science can never be regarded as absolute proof; and in the science of human nutrition the evidence is often, of necessity, indirect or even peripheral. It is legitimate as a tax-paying patron of science to complain that not enough good research into human nutrition is being done, but not legitimate to complain that what is being derived from it falls short of unequivocal certainty. Absolute certainty must forever remain an impossible ideal, to be aspired to, but never attained. As the Royal College of Physicians remarked in its report on coronary heart disease, theories at best are based upon 'a balance of probabilities'.

Chapter 4

EVERYTHING YOU EVER WANTED TO KNOW ABOUT FAT

Nutritionists have adopted very different attitudes to different classes of food; it's one of the sociological oddities of the subject. Thus with protein they began with the (correct) observation that it is essential, and then proceeded, with great conscientiousness, to find out all about it. They quickly produced all kinds of subtle concepts. that some amino acids had to be provided in the diet, for example, while some could be synthesised in the body; and showed, too, with the help of biochemists, how complicated is the life of a body protein, and how the proteins and amino acids fit in with the rest of metabolism. Although, as is related on pages 000 to 000, this zeal perhaps led the world astray for a time, it was not in itself bad. To ask what a nutrient is for, how it works, how the body deals with it, and what are the best sources of it, is the proper way to proceed.

But contrast this with their attitude to fat. In essence, what is true of protein is true of fat. It is theoretically possible to be fat-deficient, just as it is theoretically possible to be protein-deficient. More, some of the fatty acids (which are what fats are constructed from) are essential to body function, and some of these are essential in another sense, in that they must be supplied ready-made in the food. Exactly the same is true, as is noted on page 114, of amino acids.

But there are some highly significant differences between fat and proteins, and one of them is that the body does not store excess protein. Excess protein may not be good for you but at least it does not hang around in the body. Protein that is not immediately needed is degraded: the excess nitrogen is removed and excreted in the urine, and the bit that is left (the carbon) is dragooned into the general metabolism.

But of course excess fat is stored. Indeed, most of the things that the body eats that are made of carbon may eventually be turned into fat, and stored. Furthermore, various kinds of fat, and particularly crystals of cholesterol, turn up in places where they are particularly unwelcome – notably in the lining of the arteries.

So, much of the standard nutritional literature does not deal with the physiology and biochemistry of fat, as it deals with the physiology and biochemistry of protein. It does not dwell upon its merits, or its subtleties. Instead it homes in only on the pathology of fat – what happens when you have too much of the wrong kinds.

This reversal of emphasis seems to me a pity. It's a pity because nutritional advice ought to be based on deep knowledge of how each nutrient works; and 'deep knowledge', in the case of fats, is at best patchy. It's a pity too from the point of view of people trying to learn something about nutritional ideas: how can anybody make sense of exhortations to eat more polyunsaturated fat, if there is no intimation of what that fat does? Without rationale, long words have the ring of mumbo jumbo. It's also very possibly a pity because the fine chemistry of fats may yet prove to be far more significant that most nutritionists have yet got round to admitting. It may be that the present attempts to increase the fat supplies of the world (by growing more palm oil, for example, and increasing dairy herds) will prove to be misguided, and that the western world at least should be striving not to supply fat in general, but to step up supplies of just a few particular fats, some of which, at present, are none too common. I say 'western world' because fat may be a godsend, as a source of energy, for people who are undernourished. I say 'may' because the evidence that westerners are short of particular fats just isn't there. But the general observation that the biology of fats has been neglected, except by a few pioneers, and that present nutritional advice on fat really does need firming up, is incontrovertible.

So, before we look at the advice on fats that has come from official bodies these past few years, we will look briefly at what is known of the chemistry and biology of fat. The following few paragraphs are not intended to be advice; it is premature to offer nutritional advice about particular fatty acids, which is why official bodies have not done so. But they are intended to give a clue as to what some of the present discussions concerning fat are about.

What are the fats?

Fats are astonishingly varied. Suet is fat. Olive oil is fat. Beeswax is fat. The soft underlay beneath the skin of human beings, in some contexts alluring and in others repellent, is fat. Cholesterol is fat.

These diverse materials are variations on a very simple theme. All organic materials are built from atoms of carbon. Fats, compared with many organic molecules, seem pretty straightforward: they consist, fundamentally, of simple chains of carbon atoms, with hydrogen atoms on each side and a fatty acid radical (shown in Figure 1 as COOH) at one end. In general a chain of carbons with COOH at the end is called a 'fatty acid'. Any molecule that contains such an arrangement may reasonably be termed a fat, or 'lipid'.

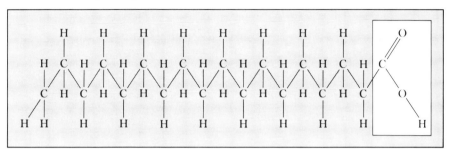

Figure 1 *The chemical structure of stearic acid, a saturated fatty acid. Note there are no double bonds between the carbon atoms.*

Variations of this simple pattern are brought about in three ways. Thus the chains may be long or short, straight or branched, saturated or unsaturated. This last source of variation seems to be the most important in nutritional terms, so it's worth asking what it implies.

Every carbon atom is able to form four chemical bonds. Hence, when carbon atoms are joined in a straight line, like beads on a string, the simplest arrangement is to use two of the bonds to link up with the carbons on either side, and to mask the two that are left with atoms of hydrogen. (They can't just be left sticking out. Nature abhors spare chemical bonds.)

This simplest of all possible arrangements is what is found in saturated fat. What the term 'saturated' alludes to, indeed, is the fact that the carbon chain is 'saturated' with hydrogen: every chemical bond that can be spared has a hydrogen stuck to it (Figure 1).

But in some fatty acids, adjacent carbons, here and there along the chain, may join to each other not by one but by two of their chemical bonds: a so-called double bond (Figure 2). Hence there are fewer

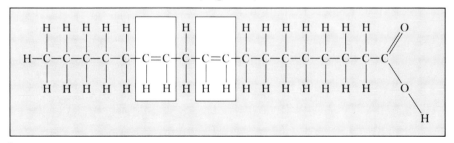

Figure 2 *The chemical structure of linoleic acid. There are two double bonds in the chain, which means that it is a polyunsaturated fatty acid (PUFA).*

chemical bonds left sticking out on either side for hydrogens to latch on to. And hence a fatty acid that includes double bonds along its length does not carry as many hydrogen atoms as is theoretically possible, and so is called 'unsaturated'. Fatty acids with only one double bond are termed 'monounsaturated', and those with two or more, 'polyunsaturated'. Polyunsaturated fatty acids are sometimes given the acronym of PUFAS.

In general, double bonds tend to be rather reactive. The double bond in unsaturated acids in particular tends to be attacked by oxygen. This innate instability is countered, in nature, by antioxidants such as vitamin E. In general, where you find a PUFA, you find a natural antioxidant.

Saturated fats tend to be harder than unsaturated fats. Thus suet is highly saturated, while fish oils tend to be unsaturated. This is just as well: a cod whose fat took the form of suet would freeze solid under the Arctic ice. However, one cannot assume that all liquid fats are polyunsaturated since some of the commonest vegetable fats, such as palm oil, are fairly saturated. But among vegetable oils, saffron, sunflower and corn oil are highly polyunsaturated.

Cholesterol is a very particular kind of fat in which the fatty acid is joined to a steroid.

So much for the glossary of terms. But what does fat actually do?

Fat as reserve energy

What most people mean by 'fat' is simply a reserve source of energy: an excellent fuel, waiting to be burnt. It is stored, in large measure, in special tissue known as adipose tissue, which lies in sheets or in mounds beneath the skin of human beings, farm animals and domestic pets, and a few wild creatures such as the seal. It also provides the marbling in red meat: even a good lean steak is remarkably fatty.

Fat is a superb source of research energy: one gram of pure fat provides about 9 kcal of energy, about twice as much as a gram of sugar or of protein. Thus a kilogram of fat can keep even a large animal going for days. Conversely, animals that do not easily accumulate fat tend to lose an enormous amount of weight when food is scarce because they are forced to burn muscle protein for energy. A red deer, for example, may lose a third of its body weight in winter.

When fat is intended only for burning, stored in droplets in the adipose tissue, its chemistry does not matter too much. The storage fat of land animals tends to be highly saturated; but if a steer is fed enormous amounts of polyunsaturated fat, then its body fat also tends to become somewhat unsaturated.

platelets, begin to aggregate. One of the things that causes them to aggregate is a substance called thromboxane, which the platelets themselves produce. It is very important that blood should clot in a wound, but undesirable that it should clot too easily since it has to circulate. In particular, it should not (as I will discuss later in more detail) form clots (thrombi) on the walls of the arteries. Accordingly, the walls of the arteries produce another substance, a prostaglandin called prostacyclin, which inhibits thromboxane. Thus whether the platelets aggregate or stick to the walls of the arteries, and so initiate blood clotting, or whether they stay separate or on the move, depends on the balance between thromboxane and prostacyclin.

In general, in most people both thromboxane and prostacyclin are synthesised from arachidonic acid – one of the EFAs in the linoleic group. However, Eskimos have very little arachidonic acid in their diet. Arachidonic acid, after all, comes largely from red meat, but the Eskimo diet is rich instead in fish. Fish oil is rich in eicosapentaenoic acid, or EPA, which is one of the linolenic group. But the human body is content to substitute EPA for arachidonic acid. Platelets proceed to synthesise thromboxane from EPA, just as they would from arachidonic acid; and the artery walls make EPA-based prostacyclin.

The only caveat is that thromboxane based on EPA does not work. It does not cause platelets to aggregate. But EPA-based prostacyclin works perfectly well. Hence, by making thromboxane and prostacyclin from EPA instead of from arachidonic acid, the whole balance of the agents that influence clotting is shifted. Hardly surprisingly, then, the blood of Eskimos does not clot as easily as that of the average European. Eskimos have, indeed, a 'bleeding tendency'.

They also have very little heart disease; and when they die, their arteries are remarkably clear, quite unlike the clogged and corrupted vessels that most of us take to our graves. It is not yet clear whether, or to what extent, differences in blood clotting account for differences in the incidence of heart attack between different populations; but it is known that blood clotting plays a significant role in generating coronary heart disease, and in precipitating heart attack. It is also clear that Eskimos have a diet very high in PUFAs. EPA might not be the only factor that saves them from heart disease but it must be considered a promising candidate.

Some nutritionists have suggested that we need not lose too much sleep over EFAs because the two basic acids from which they are made, linoleic and linolenic, are bound to be present in sufficient quantities in our diet. It's clear, though, that in the normal western diet arachidonic acid from the linoleic series tends to prevail over EPA from the linolenic series; and, in general, the seed-based linoleic series is more likely to be well represented. (Linoleic, for example, is the principal PUFA in polyunsaturated margarines.) In addition, David Horrobin has pointed out that although it is theoretically possible for different acids within any one series to be converted into one another, this does not necessarily happen in practice as freely as it should. Thus linoleic acid itself is not active in the body. It does not become active until it is converted into gammalinolenic acid (GLA). But the enzyme that effects this conversion is highly sensitive and is, for example, (and intriguingly) inhibited by saturated fat. Indeed Dr Horrobin has suggested that it is at least possible that some of the ill effects of saturated fat result from the fact that it prevents linoleic acid being converted to active forms – and thus produces a deficiency in EFAs of the linoleic series even though the diet may contain enough linoleic acid. This, of course, is speculative, but it's interesting.

However, the point of this section is not to present a panegyric to EFAs but merely to point out some of the ways in which PUFAs in general might be important. To round off these background notes we should look briefly at the final actor in the fat saga, cholesterol.

Cholesterol

Cholesterol is a highly intriguing molecule. It is synthesised in the body and turns up in various contexts which, on the face of it, have no very obvious connection one with another. Thus cholesterol is the raw material from which steroid hormones are made, of which there are many kinds with many functions, including the sex hormones. At least, cholesterol is not exactly the 'raw material', as it can itself be synthesised from simpler materials; but it is the first steroid to be synthesised, from which the others are then made.

It is from cholesterol, too, that the bile salts are formed. The bile salts are synthesised in the liver, stored in the gall bladder, and pass down the bile duct into the small intestine, where they play a part in breaking up fats into small drops (emulsifying them, that is) to aid in their digestion and absorption. When the bile salts have completed this task they pass down the gut into the colon, where they are in large part re-absorbed. We will explore this further on page 103, in the discussion of dietary fibre.

Surplus cholesterol is excreted in the bile. If there is too much of it, or if the chemistry of the bile salts has been altered, then the cholesterol may crystallise to form gallstones.

Cholesterol is not allowed to circulate in the body unchaperoned. When it is carried through the blood, it is for the most part attached to protein, and in such form is referred to as a lipoprotein (a fat-protein). Lipoproteins take various forms. In one form there is a great deal of lipid and very little protein; in another, somewhat more protein; and in a third type, there is more protein than lipid. Lipids are light (fats are lighter than water) and so the lipoproteins with a high proportion of lipid are less dense than those with a preponderance of protein. Hence the three classes of lipoprotein are called very-low-density lipoproteins (VLDLs); low-density lipoproteins (LDLs) and high-density lipoproteins (HDLs). For the purposes of discussion I will consider the VLDLs and LDLs as one category (that is, as LDLs) and will refer to them all, in future, only by their initials.

In general, it seems that LDLs represent cholesterol on its way into the tissues, while HDL represents cholesterol being carried to the liver for the purpose of excretion. The importance of LDLs and HDLs in disease will be considered later.

The need for knowledge

This, then, is some of the very basic biology of fats. One day, beyond doubt, knowledge of fat metabolism, and of the effects of diet on health and disease, will be so detailed that nutritional advice will follow from physiological knowledge as night follows day. At present this is not the case. At present it is not clear, for example, whether the influence of particular EFAs on blood clotting does have any profound effects on the well-being of most people most of the time. At present, indeed, dietary advice is based principally on observed relationships between diets and patterns of disease.

However, the detailed knowledge of fat metabolism now emerging is profoundly important in nutritional lore for three reasons. Firstly it suggests areas that ought to be investigated further – and which might in the future form the basis for detailed nutritional advice. Secondly, detailed knowledge at the very least helps to show which dietary hypotheses are plausible, and which are less so. Thirdly, the picture that is now emerging of the astonishing intricacies of fat metabolism is in itself salutory: it shows how delicate are the mechanisms that we daily assail with massive infusions of fat with very little thought for its origin and even less for the subtleties of its chemistry.

But now we must leave speculative musings and ask what various expert committees have concluded is a proper and healthy intake of fat. The first question of all, perhaps, is why anyone might suppose there is anything wrong with what we are doing now?

Chapter 5

WHAT'S WRONG WITH FAT?

There has not been a learned committee on nutrition in general, or its effect on heart disease in particular, that has not homed in upon fat. The crude observation is that societies that on average eat a lot of fat have a much higher incidence of certain diseases than societies that eat a little fat. And those diseases, in particular, are cancer of the breast, cancer of the colon and coronary heart disease (sometimes abbreviated to CHD). That observation in itself does not prove anything (and, as we saw in Chapter 3, 'proof' is always a very delicate concept in science), but it should arouse attention; and has indeed done so.

Of the three diseases, CHD has caused the greatest alarm, not especially for the male chauvinist reason that it affects far more men than women (certainly before the age of 65), but because it really has become an astonishingly common disease. In the UK, cardiovascular disease (which includes stroke, as well as CHD) accounts for more than half the deaths of men aged between 45 and 54, and three quarters of those cardiovascular deaths are caused by CHD. Various cancers are the next greatest single cause of mortality within men of that age group, but account for only 26 per cent of deaths. In other western countries CHD may not occur quite so frequently (indeed, parts of the UK are now the world leaders in the CHD stakes) but it is invariably the greatest single cause of death among men who should be in their peak years – 'peak' at least in terms of earning power and responsibility.

Of course, a mere association between high fat intake and a high rate of CHD does not prove that a high fat intake *causes* heart disease. Societies with a high rate of CHD also tend to watch more television, for example (although the correlation between CHD and television is nothing like so strong as the correlation between CHD and fat). But although one might suggest that too much TV may predispose to CHD (after all, it is a very sedentary occupation) no-one would suggest that the cause is direct, because there is no obvious way in which watching a screen *could* cause the changes in the blood vessels that lead to CHD. The crude observation that societies with a high intake of fat tend to have a lot of CHD, however, is not only somewhat less crude than I have suggested, but also accords with a great many other observations, some of which suggest that there are very clear ways in which a high fat intake could indeed damage the arteries.

So with CHD we have a rounded story: a clear correlation between fat intake and disease, and several ideas about how one might lead to the other. With the various cancers associated with fat the picture is not so clear. It is reasonable, therefore, to concentrate this discussion on CHD. After all, if CHD, breast cancer and cancer of the colon really do have a common factor in fat, then reducing fat intake to reduce one disease should help to reduce all three.

What is coronary heart disease?

The heart is a bag of muscle, pumping away 40 to 100 or more times a minute depending on whether you are say, Bjorn Borg or, a marginally less fit writer of books on nutrition. The heart is constantly full of blood, which on the face of it should keep it supplied with the oxygen and nutrients it needs. But the muscle of a human heart is far too thick to derive oxygen and nutrient from the blood that's just passing through its chambers. The heart muscle needs a blood supply of its own. And this it has in the form of an artery that encircles it. Indeed, the form of this artery was compared by early anatomists to a crown which, to quote Shakespeare's Richard II, 'rounds the mortal temples of a king'. Hence they named it the 'coronary artery'. (And there, to continue the prophetic words of King Richard, 'keeps death his court'.)

Arteries are astonishingly complex structures. They need to be. They must provide a smooth surface for the blood to run over and to prevent it clotting, which it has a constant tendency to do. They must provide this surface despite being abraded and buffeted by the viscous blood itself, and bend this way and that as the body moves. They must resist the constant changing of pressure within them as the heart pumps, and help the blood on its way by recoiling energetically as the blood surges through them. They have, accordingly (as designed by nature at least), a silken-smooth lining known as the endothelium; thick layers outside that of smooth muscle and connective tissue, which together form the media; and on the outside, for good measure, a sheath of connective tissue housing nerves and subsidiary blood vessels to supply the muscle fibres of the media.

Most animals and some human beings die at the end of their allotted span with their arteries as neat as nature conceived them to be, although, inevitably, in older animals and humans the collagen fibres lose some of their elasticity, so that the arteries stiffen, just as the skin stiffens. But in most human beings, as time goes on, other changes occur which are not simply the result of growing older. In particular, areas of the arterial walls become thickened and rough: the thick rough areas are called plaques. The condition in which plaques accumulate is called atheroma.

The precise way in which plaques form; exactly what kind of damage triggers the whole process off; and how it proceeds and at what pace – all this is still a subject for discussion. It is simply not possible to cut up human beings at intervals throughout their lives to see exactly what is happening to their arteries and at what times, which is the only definitive way to trace the exact sequence of events. But the kinds of things that happen are roughly as follows.

First, it seems, there is some kind of damage to the lining of the artery – the endothelium. This, at least, was suggested by the great 19th-century German pathologist, Rudolf Virchow. In fact, such damage may not be the first thing that happens, and may not be necessary in order for plaques to start building up; but Virchow's idea remains sound, and is supported by common sense and some experimental evidence.

Damage to the endothelium brings circulating blood in direct contact with the layers beneath. These are not designed to allow blood to run smoothly over them, and probably not so able to prevent clotting as is the endothelium.

Then, at the site of damage, there is a build-up of a great variety of local tissues. The plaque that is eventually formed contains connective tissue and muscle fibres from the wall of the arteries; clotted blood; calcium (the plaque may become chalky); and fat. In particular, the plaque is dotted with crystals of cholesterol.

There is evidence, however, that this pile-up of tissue is not a crude accumulation, like debris collecting in a drain when its wall is cracked. Earl P Benditt at the University of Washington School of Medicine has shown that the atheromatous plaque is, in effect, a benign tumour. He has shown, indeed, that the tissue which sets the pace in the formation of a plaque is the smooth muscle from the media. His experiments indicate that at some point a single cell within the media begins to divide, and divide again, exactly as occurs in a tumour; and that the other cells and materials found in the plaque then accumulate around this proliferating mass of muscle cells. I include this very brief reference to Professor Benditt's work not simply because it is interesting, but because it shows very clearly that atheroma really is a complex disease; the arteries do not simply 'fur up', like a kettle. The point is that medical science is still a long way from explaining precisely what does happen in the build-up of atheroma, and why; and whatever definitive theory finally emerges (as surely it will) it must take account of Benditt's observations.

When the final theory is produced it may well show that cholesterol in particular is a key factor in precipitating the course of events; and this, indeed, is implicit in today's nutritional theories. But the final theory will not suggest that the body is so badly designed that fat simply accumulates on the inside of the arteries, like gunge in a drain-pipe. Whatever the role of cholesterol is in damaging arteries, it is subtle.

The second reason for mentioning Benditt's work is that there has been much discussion as to whether plaques can actually grow smaller, once they have formed (apart, that is, from being removed surgically, which indeed is possible). In general, there are some reasons for thinking some reduction is possible, especially if the plaque is not too well advanced. But when we consider that the plaque is not simply a squidge of fat, but is structured, with a multiplicity of cells, the hopes for radical reduction (except by surgery) become more remote. Prevention has to be the name of the game.

Anyway, changes in the arteries of western human beings begin to take place before people reach the first decade. It is not clear whether these early, fatty changes inevitably lead to full-blown atheroma, but the fact is that damage can begin early. By middle age, especially in men, atheroma is well advanced. Of particular importance are the plaques that build up in the coronary artery. The coronary artery becomes narrower and narrower. The narrowing of the artery can obviously impair the function of the heart, and may (though it also may not) cause pain, known as angina; but just because you are free of pain, it does not mean you are safe. Eventually a blood clot may block the tiny passage that remains in the coronary artery. The section of the heart served by that particular section of artery finds itself without blood supply, and stops beating. This upsets the rhythm of the entire heart, and the result is heart attack. Heart attacks are not invariably fatal (though more than half prove to be so within a month), but after recovery an area of heart muscle, deprived of its blood supply, may remain as a wedge of dead tissue known as an 'infarct'.

It is sometimes suggested that the reason western people have such a high incidence of heart attack when East African villagers, say, generally do not, is that westerners live longer. It is true that the longer you live the more likely you are to have a heart attack, and that people who die of infection before the age of 40 are therefore liable to escape this condition. But when people from aboriginal societies die at the age of 40 or so, their arteries prove, at autopsy, to be clean as a flute; as smooth and undamaged as the arteries of a western five-year-old. There is absolutely no reason to assume that such people would suffer heart attacks, however long they lived.

Cholesterol and CHD

The fact that atheromatous plaques tend to contain crystals of cholesterol should raise the alert about fat (we really cannot afford to ignore any clues), but it obviously does not prove, or come near to proving, that cholesterol causes the damage in the first place. Indeed one American pathologist, Hans Kaunitz, has pointed out that cholesterol in atheromatous plaques may simply be an innocent by-stander (a stranger caught up in the crowd) or may even be contributing to the repair of the damaged tissue. However, there are other reasons for thinking that the role of cholesterol is less than innocent, and among these are the increasingly powerful contributions from epidemiology: the study of the distribution of diseases.

One of the seminal studies was by the American physiologist Ansel Keys in the 1960s. He and his colleagues studied the life-style of people in seven different nations that had very different levels of heart attack, ranging from the United States and Finland, with very high rates of heart attack, to Japan, Yugoslavia and Crete, with low rates. Others since have also pursued this kind of study, and always the same kind of picture emerges. There is a range of factors correlating with a high incidence of heart attack, and chief among these 'risk factors' are the big three – smoking, hypertension and a high concentration of cholesterol in the blood. We will discuss what is meant by 'risk factor' in slightly more detail later on and also look at a few risk factors not on that list. But first we should look specifically at blood cholesterol.

The point can perhaps best be made by comparing just two countries, South Japan and East Finland. East Finland is no longer top of the grisly world league of heart disease (that position is now held by Scotland), but it was in the 1970s. In the most notorious of the Finnish regions, North Karelia, there were 1000 heart attacks among 180,000 people in 1972. That's just in one year; and of course the 180,000 included women, who do not suffer as many heart attacks as men, and children. I have, incidentally, visited schools in North Karelia where one third of the children were without fathers – fathers lost not through war, but through coronary heart disease. In South Japan, however, heart attack is rare.

Within all societies, the concentrations of cholesterol in the blood follows quite a wide range, but most people tend towards some 'average' figure. As shown in Figure 3, in South Japan the lowest concentrations of cholesterol found are about 80 mg per 100 ml of blood serum (a figure

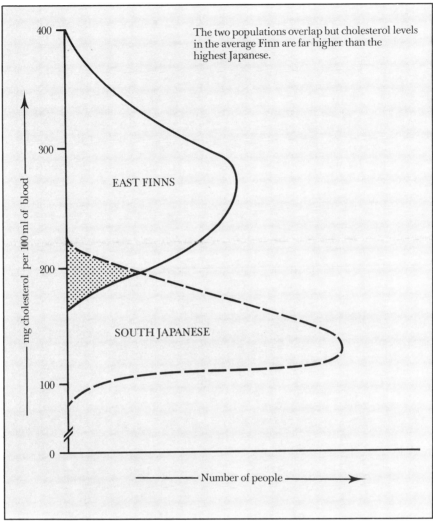

Figure 3 *The average concentration of cholesterol in the blood of East Finns and Southern Japanese. The two populations overlap but cholesterol levels in the average Finn are far higher than in the* highest *Japanese.*

generally abbreviated to '80 mg per cent'). The highest is around 220 mg per cent. Most people have about 120 mg per cent.

But in East Finland the *lowest* levels are around 160 mg per cent – notably higher than the majority of South Japanese. The highest levels in Finns are around 400 mg per cent, while most hover at around 270 mg per cent. Thus the *majority* in Finland have higher cholesterol levels than the highest level that occurs in the Japanese.

Of course, if the comparison had been done only with this one factor, and only two nations had been compared, then the figures would mean nothing at all. It would be pointed out that there is also a difference in temperature between the two countries, that the winters are longer in Finland, that the Japanese have slanting eyes and spend more time squatting on their haunches – all these and a hundred other differences. But many nations have been compared and many different factors within those nations: every factor, indeed, that can conceivably be measured. And always the same picture has emerged. When the concentration of cholesterol within the blood is high, the level of heart attack is high. Moreover, in general, the higher the level, the greater the incidence of coronary heart disease. Furthermore (a point which I feel is the most telling of all), wherever the concentration of serum cholesterol is very low – around 120 mg cholesterol per cent – then coronary heart disease virtually does not exist. And, as the World Health Organisation Expert Committee put the matter in their report of 1982, *Prevention of Coronary Heart Disease* (p. 17): 'The Expert Committee know of no population in whom CHD is common that does not also have a relatively high mean level of total cholesterol' – where 'relatively high' meant around 200 mg per cent in adults.

Of course, if you were simply comparing Finns with Japanese, then you could argue that there is a pretty obvious genetic difference between the two. However, when Japanese go to live in America (and there are many Japanese in California) their level of heart diseases inexorably edges up towards that of the rest of America. And, of course, the same kind of argument applies equally to blacks, who suffer few heart attacks in African villages, but as many as anybody else in the USA.

Then again, *within* any one population people with high concentrations of serum cholesterol can be seen to run a greater risk of CHD than people with less cholesterol in their blood. Thus one of the most famous (and important) studies of heart disease in the world has been taking place in Framingham near Boston in the USA since the 1940s. There a team of medical scientists has measured just about everything measurable on just about everybody. Some people have now been monitored since infancy and the measurements correlated with their subsequent fate. The men of Framingham aged 55 and over have serum cholesterol concentrations ranging from about 140 or so up to around 400, with most teetering around 220 to 250 mg per cent. As you can see from Figure 4, the chances of death from heart attack increase steadily as cholesterol concentration increases.

This relationship between concentration of blood cholesterol and chances of heart attack merits four qualifying paragraphs.

The first, as was pointed out by the Royal College of Physicians in their report, *Prevention of Coronary Heart Disease* (1976), is that the risk to

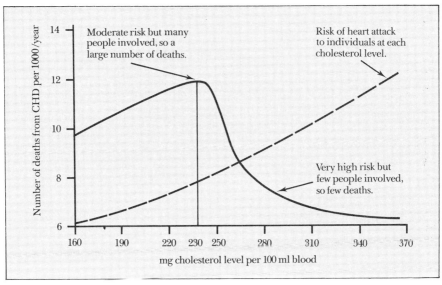

Figure 4 *As the blood cholesterol level goes up, the risk of heart attack in each individual increases. However, few people have very high blood cholesterol. So most deaths occur among people with 'average' cholesterol levels, simply because far more people fall into this category. (Based on statistics from studies on heart disease carried out in Framingham, Mass., USA.)*

an individual increases enormously as the concentration rises. You might suppose that a man with 350 mg cholesterol per cent would run twice the risk of a heart attack as a man with 175 mg. But in fact he runs about five times the risk. (There are, too, a few unfortunate people with a particular genetic defect that produces blood cholesterol levels of 1000 per cent or more. Heart attack in such people is almost inevitable, and common before the age of 30. Because this is a very particular disease it may not be relevant to the population as a whole; but the observation stands, for what it is worth.)

Secondly, note that there is virtually no-one in Britain or the US (with the possible exception of some lifelong vegans) whose blood cholesterol levels are so low that they can consider themselves safe from coronary heart disease. Britons with 200 mg cholesterol per cent may consider their level is 'low'; and so it is compared to most other Britons. But note how high this 'low' figure is compared to the 'safe' levels of rural Japanese (120 mg per cent). Note, too, that the average figure – around 230 mg per cent in Britain – is far higher than is desirable. In short, we are all of us at risk. We should all of us take precautions. The Royal College of Physicians recognised, however, that for practical purposes doctors should identify patients who were particularly at risk; and they felt that anyone with blood cholesterol higher than around 275 mg per cent should be exhorted to take dietary and other advice very seriously indeed. But the physicians stressed that they did not mean to imply that anyone below this arbitrary figure of 275 mg per cent should consider themselves safe. It's just that the people above that level are particularly unsafe.

Thirdly – and this point follows from the one before – note the shape of the graph that shows the number of men in Framingham with each particular concentration of cholesterol. Men with 350 mg or so per cent of serum may be individually at very high risk – but there are few of them. Men with 'only' 230 or so mg per cent are at much less risk individually – but there are millions of them. Thus, in countries such as the UK, USA, or Finland, most heart attacks occur among people who have blood cholesterol levels that are 'average' for each country – around 230 mg per cent.

The *individual risk* is far lower at 230 mg per cent than at 300 mg or more, but the total *number* of incidents if far greater. There is a deeply deceptive tendency to confuse the word 'average' with the word 'normal'. Thus one famous American heart surgeon has been known to comment that he does not believe that CHD has anything much to do with blood cholesterol levels because most of his patients have 'normal' concentrations of blood cholesterol. An equally famous epidemiologist pointed out, however, (although I paraphrase) that such an argument is no more than a deeply deceptive, and highly dangerous, play on words. We should rather argue that it is not 'normal' to have a heart attack. We might therefore more reasonably argue that a 'normal' level of blood cholesterol is one that does not lead to heart attack, which does not mean 230 mg per cent, but nearer 130. What is average, or common, in the USA, UK, or Finland, is in this sense anything but normal. Most of our arteries (and blood lipid profiles) belong in textbooks of pathology.

The final conditional clause concerns the distinction between LDLs and HDLs. In general, as I briefly mentioned in Chapter 4, LDLs represent cholesterol on its way in, and HDLs represent cholesterol on the way out. In general, too, there is evidence that HDL concentration is *inversely* related to the chances of heart attack. So if you have high HDLs, you are less likely to have a heart attack. In theory, then, someone with very high *total* cholesterol (and all the figures we have given relate to total cholesterol) could be very safe indeed – provided that most of the cholesterol was HDL. In practice, however, HDL cholesterol makes up only about 20–30 per cent of total cholesterol, so, in general, as the World Health Organisation pointed out in its own report on *Prevention of Coronary Heart Disease* (1982), a high total cholesterol remains undesirable because only a minority of the total will be made up of beneficial HDLs. However, it does seem to be a good thing, in general, for individuals to try to boost their own HDLs – or, more precisely, to increase the ratio of HDLs to LDLs. As I will explain below, exercise tends to increase HDLs, and so do polyunsaturated fats.

We are still left with a key question. In general, the epidemiological evidence does indicate that a high risk of heart attack is correlated with a high level of cholesterol in the blood. But that still does not mean that the high cholesterol is *causing* the heart attacks. There could be something going on in the body which damages the arteries, thus leading to heart attack, which also – quite by chance – raises blood cholesterol as well. It could be, as Dr Kaunitz suggested, that cholesterol is an innocent by-stander.

To be sure, this particular ghost has not been definitively laid. High blood cholesterol could simply be a litmus, indicating that some disease is in progress, but not necessarily influencing the course of the disease itself. However, there are several reasons, for not taking that purist view. One is that there is independent evidence that high levels of cholesterol can lead to the kind of damage which develops into atheroma (or at least into atheroma-like lesions); or that high levels of cholesterol can exacerbate damage already in existence. This has been shown many times by experiments on animals, for example. (Of course you can argue that animals are not humans, and indeed point out with justice that the kinds of lesions produced in the arteries of experimental animals are far from identical with human atheroma.)

It seems to me to be absolutely proper that this argument should continue. So long as there is a shadow of a reasonable doubt that high blood cholesterol causes atheroma, then scientists, somewhere, should be investigating the point. If cholesterol is not the cause of the damage, after all, then we are missing something else. However, no matter how much evidence is accrued on this point, it is hard to see how it could ever be shown definitively, ie beyond the point of argument, that cholesterol is a principal cause of damage to the arteries. In the meantime, there are plenty of, albeit imperfect, snippets of evidence to suggest that it is an important cause, and those snippets are supported by common sense. In the meantime, too, people continue to die at a horrendous rate from heart attack, and it is incumbent on physicians to give advice on how to try and avoid this fate. At the moment the advice of learned committees (such as the World Health Organisation and the Royal College of Physicians) is based largely on the proposition that high blood cholesterol does help to cause atheroma, and hence heart attack; and this proposition is based on what the Royal College of Physicians termed 'the balance of probabilities'.

If, then, we accept as reasonable the proposition that high blood cholesterol is itself damaging, and not simply indicative of some deeper, darker process, we must ask a further question. What causes blood cholesterol levels to rise?

Why do some people have high blood cholesterol?
No-one would deny that the concentration of cholesterol in your blood is to a large extent determined by your genes. The point is not that there is an important genetic difference between races (we have covered that point: Japanese, Africans and Caucasians on the same kinds of diet finish up with much the same kind of blood cholesterol levels), but that there are large genetic differences between *individuals* of the same race. Thus some Japanese on their daily diet of rice, seaweed and radishes or whatever finish up with only 80 or so mg per cent cholesterol in their blood; while others on the same diet finish up with 160 or so. Similarly, though many Finns have cholesterol levels over 300 mg per cent, others with much the same lifestyle stay at around 200.

However, there can be very little doubt that environment also influences blood cholesterol levels. We have covered that point too: a Japanese in Japan (with a traditional Japanese lifestyle) will only rarely have blood cholesterol above 180 mg per cent; while the same Japanese in California, if he lives there a long time, will be lucky to get below 200 mg per cent.

So it's worth asking what it is about lifestyle that makes the difference. Again, if you just compare Finns with traditional Japanese you are lost: there are a hundred and one differences in ways of life. But if you compare the broad pattern of nations, then the item which correlates almost precisely with high blood cholesterol is diet. And of all the differences in diet which exist, the one that correlates best, both with general blood levels of cholesterol and with general level of heart attack, is fat. We find, in general, that societies obtaining 40 per cent or more of their calories from fat – societies, that is, such as Britain – have a high incidence of CHD. Those societies that obtain less than 20 per cent of their calories from fat (like the traditional Japanese) have virtually no CHD at all. Those with an in-between level of fat intake, such as the people of Greece, Yugoslavia, or southern Italy – all people, in fact, on a 'Mediterranean' diet – have low levels of heart attack, which increase the more fat they eat. Thus, traditionally, there was less heart attack in Naples in the south of Italy than in Bologna in the north. The southerners had a low-fat, high-carbohydrate diet: the northerners moved more quickly towards the 'affluent', high-fat diet more characteristic of northern Europe.

Many have, very properly, noted the shortcomings of this kind of statistic. Some have pointed out, for example, that the correlation between a high fat intake and a high incidence of heart attack is far from exact. For example, Eskimos clearly have a very high fat intake (they are virtually carnivores, after all) and so, it's suggested, do the Masai in Africa, who live off the products of their cattle. However, there are good reasons for thinking that both the Eskimos and the Masai are special cases. The Eskimos, for example, as I mentioned in Chapter 4, have a diet very high in polyunsaturates, which tend to lower total blood cholesterol and to raise HDLs. And, as noted in the same chapter, the Eskimos' extraordinarily high intake of the particular PUFA, eicosapentaenoic acid, reduces the tendency of their blood to form thrombi. The details of Masai diet do not seem to be well known: but anecdotal evidence suggests that the total calorific intake is so low that they are simply not in the same dietary category as people in the affluent, urban world.

In general, we may concede that Eskimos and Masai seem, on the face of it, anomalous and also that these people ideally should be investigated further (although they must be tired by now of being prodded by scientists). But these two (and a few other) apparent exceptions are not enough to detract from the very reasonable supposition that a high-fat diet does indeed result, in general, in a high concentration of blood cholesterol.

Some detractors have pointed out that within any one population there seems to be no very consistent difference between the fat intake of people with the highest levels of blood cholesterol, and those with the lowest. Finnish lumberjacks with 350 mg cholesterol per cent traditionally ate sausages all day on bread spread thickly with butter ('they don't butter their bread,' it used to be said, 'they bread their butter'). But those with only 200 mg per cent ate more or less the same. Here we come back to the point that there are significant genetic differences between individuals within the same population.

The point is, in fact, that genetic differences between individuals can and almost certainly do account for the fact that two individuals who take the same amount of fat may have different amounts of cholesterol in their blood. But genetic differences do not account for the fact that whole populations of people who consistently eat little fat have lower levels of blood cholesterol than people in societies who eat a great deal of fat. This kind of point can be difficult to grasp, but once you see it, it's obvious. An analogy with sun-tan may help. In the sun, some *bona fide* white Caucasians quickly acquire a serviceable tan, while others with the same exposure go pink and then peel. The difference is genetic: some people have a greater ability to manufacture the necessary skin pigments. On the other hand, when white Caucasians work in sunny countries they tend on average (even the ones who initially go pink) to become browner than those left at home. Clearly there is a genetic difference, even with Caucasians, in the response to sunlight: but no-one would doubt that sunlight does actually *cause* sun-tan.

Again, the idea that high fat intake actually causes high blood cholesterol is enhanced by various kinds of observation, including experiments on animals. Again, one can argue that animals are not humans. Again, in the end, one has to admit that there is no absolute proof of cause and effect, and cannot be. But again one must ask whether it is worth abandoning what seems like a strong idea, or failing to act upon it, for the sake of a rather dubious brand of intellectual puritanism.

The nature of the fat is important

We have seen already in Chapter 4 that the metabolism of fat is immensely complicated, and that the details of all the effects of different kinds of fat upon the body are far from being established. Nevertheless, it is known that different classes of fat have different effects on blood cholesterol levels. Thus, saturated fat in the diet tends to increase blood cholesterol. A high dietary intake of cholesterol itself also tends to increase blood cholesterol; but PUFAs in the diet tend to reduce blood cholesterol. Monounsaturated fatty acids seem to be neutral in their effect on blood cholesterol, neither raising nor lowering it: and monounsaturates include olive oil, one of the principal sources of fat in the traditional Mediterranean diet.

Various expert committees in recent years (the Royal College of Physicians, the McGovern Committee in the USA, the World Health Organisation and NACNE* among them) have each drawn attention to the effects of the different classes of fat on dietary cholesterol. But the different committees have differed somewhat in the nature of the advice they have given; and other experts have independently added their own voices to the discussion. Again, it's not the function of this book simply to add another formula to the plethora already in existence, but it is in our brief to make a quick tour of the kinds of ideas that the experts are taking into account.

The expert committees in general, and most independent experts for good measure, tend to recommend reducing the total intake of fat. They differ in the precise amounts, but their line of reasoning tends to be much the same. In general, if westerners (i e North Americans and Europeans) could push their total fat intake down toward the traditional Mediterranean–Japanese levels of 20 per cent, then coronary heart

* National Advisory Committee on Nutrition Education.

disease would become rare. In general, however (the expert committees tend to admit), people brought up in our fat-orientated society are unlikely to change so radically, so some kind of compromise is called for. Thus the Royal College of Physicians in Britain suggested reducing fat intake to around 35 per cent of total calories, while the McGovern Committee suggested 30 per cent. For individuals who do not want to walk around with pocket calculators, a general shift from fatty meals to those high in unrefined carbohydrate is the general, most widely agreed-upon order of the day.

Expert committees and individual experts differ somewhat in their emphasis on PUFAS. In general, as I have noted, detailed knowledge of exactly how PUFAS behave is not yet forthcoming. In general, too, as we noted in the very first chapter, it does not seem wise to advise people to enter uncharted nutritional waters and to take up a diet that has not been taken up and well tried in the past. Eskimos aside, the effects of diets very high in PUFAS in general on large populations over long periods are not well known. Thus, while there are some individuals who regard PUFAS as elixirs and recommend taking daily draughts, expert committees recommend a more modest shift of emphasis. Thus the Royal College of Physicians suggested 'partial replacement' of saturated fats by PUFAS. Exactly what this implies in dietary terms we will examine later.

Experts have also differed in their advice on dietary cholesterol. No-one doubts that diets high in cholesterol can raise serum cholesterol levels. Foods high in cholesterol include eggs and liver, the highest levels of all being found in brains and some fish roes (which, of course, are eggs). Most people eat eggs, and some people eat a great many of them, but few people eat brains very often; so, in practice, eggs tend to be by far the biggest single source of cholesterol.

In general, then, it seems to make sense to cut out eggs. This, indeed, is how many American experts have argued. Thus Dr Jeremiah Stamler, chairman of the Department of Community Health and Preventive Medicine at Northwestern University Medical School, Illinois, USA, has been heard to suggest on networked television, that 'the less eggs eaten the better. And none isn't bad'.

Dr William Castelli, one of the directors of the Framingham heart study, also has a down on eggs. He points out that the cholesterol in the egg is in the yolk and advocates eating only the white, if an egg is what you feel you have got to have.

But then Dr Castelli is fond of relating the bad old days of American high living during the period after World War II, when many Americans, with the memory both of war and of the depression still with them, were tasting affluence for the first time, and when US agriculture was coming into full flood. Then, says Dr Castelli, roadside cafes tended to advertise six-egg breakfasts; or 32-ounce steaks with as many eggs as you could eat thrown in.

Britain's Royal College of Physicians perhaps had more modest memories of eggs. In any case, they pointed out in their report that dietary cholesterol is certainly not in itself desirable, but that the average Briton does not actually eat much of it. Indeed, the average daily intake is around 500 mg (half a gram) compared with more than 100 grams of total fats, which include more than 50 grams of saturated fat. The physicians also pointed out that absorption of cholesterol tends to go down as intake goes up. Thus they did not feel it was really worthwhile offering specific recommendation to reduce cholesterol intake – or not, at least, to the population at large; they did suggest though, in a general way, that we should eat 'fewer egg yolks'. (It's worth bearing in mind, too, that eggs do not manifest only as eggs, or indeed as omelettes. They are widely used in cooking, not least in cakes and batters.)

I have always felt myself (as I explained at length in *Future Cook*, Mitchell Beazley, London, 1980) that the best advice is not to strive officiously to cut out all saturated fat or cholesterol, but to make sure that the saturated fat and cholesterol you do eat is a genuine treat. It's the gratuitous use of fat that's harmful; and if the six-egg breakfast is a thing of the past, the sweet biscuits heavy with lard, the sauces clagged with butter, the highly saturated and highly deceptive brands of margarine, and the cheapo sausage, are still very much with us.

But we will be returning to the niceties of diet. A brief word, first, about what is meant by 'risk factor', and about some of the other risk factors, besides dietary fats.

Risk factors and healthy living

If you had asked any good country doctor in the past 300 years what you should do to stay healthy, he would have told you much the same kind of things as are advocated by today's medical scientists. He would not, probably, have placed specific emphasis of the dangers of fat or salt (perhaps even the opposite) but he would have told you not to eat too much, and not to get fat. He would possibly even have advocated the odd glass of wine, while warning against over-indulgence, and spoken in favour of brisk walks. He would also have told you not to worry too much, or get over-excited. So what, you might ask, is new? Why decorate good sound common sense with talk of 'risk factors' and convoluted physiology?

The difference between the new and the old is that the new is more specific and more firmly based. Generalisations are fine (if they are the right generalisations), but they are also fragile unless supported by evidence and argument. Thus, the same 18th-century physician who advised you, very properly, to take brisk walks and to avoid getting drunk, would also have drained away half your blood to get rid of infections. The moral is that even when advice seems good, ancient or modern, it's worth asking what it's based upon.

In practice, 18th-century medical lore was based, at its best, on common sense, personal experience and tradition. Modern medical advice on the specific matter of coronary heart disease is based on the concept of risk factors, and on the idea that it's a good thing to reduce those risk factors. So we should not only ask what is meant by 'risk factors', but also whether it is possible to reduce them and, if so, whether that is in practice a useful thing to do.

Risk factors are characteristics, or ways of life, that are not only associated with particular diseases, but also apparently help to cause them. In the case of CHD, the three outstanding risk factors, among the general population, are high blood cholesterol, hypertension and smoking. Each of these three factors multiplies the effects of the others. Thus you could double your risk of heart attack by smoking. You could also double it if your blood pressure was raised. And you could double it, too, if your cholesterol was high. But if you had all of these disadvantages – and each to a degree that by itself would double your risk – then you would increase your chances of heart attack $2 \times 2 \times 2 = 8$ times.

Of these three outstanding risk factors, high blood cholesterol is the only one likely to lead to heart attack all by itself. People with very high blood cholesterol levels may suffer CHD even if their blood pressure is low and they do smoke. But people with very low blood cholesterol who have high blood pressure do not, in general, have CHD, although they are prone to stroke, the condition in which a blood vessel ruptures in the brain. (Thus traditional Japanese have a low incidence of CHD, but a high incidence of stroke.)

These three risk factors are not, of course, the only three. Coronary heart disease is *par excellence* a 'multifactorial disease'; many different factors compound to produce it although, as we have seen, high blood cholesterol is the one that in the end is crucial. But there are several good reasons why high blood cholesterol, hypertension and smoking have been singled out from all the others. For one thing, each of these three factors seems to cause the disease to a greater extent than the others. High blood cholesterol seems, among other things, to help build up the atheroma. Hypertension may help to damage the lining of the arteries.

Smoking (among other things) may upset the rhythm of the heart and so precipitate heart attack in people whose coronary arteries are already damaged. If these factors did not contribute in a direct physiological way to causing CHD, then they could not properly be called risk factors.

Statistics suggest that another risk factor is living in an area where the water is soft, rather than where it is hard. Evidently the balance of metal ions in hard water has effects on cell membranes that in general favour heart function. But the influence of hardness of water is small compared to the big three risk factors. It's worth mentioning, but it is only gilt on the lily.

There are yet other risk factors that do have a very big effect, but are not of general importance. Thus diabetics, at least in western societies, tend to run a high risk of CHD. So diabetes is a big risk factor, but obviously not one which applies to the population at large.

Obesity is a most interesting case. In general, a 45-year-old man of average height who weighs 15 stone runs a greater risk of heart attack than a man of the same age and height who weighs only 11 stone. But the point here is that people who are overweight may at some time in their lives have eaten a lot (including a lot of fat) and may well, therefore, have high blood cholesterol. They are also more likely to be sedentary than slimmer people. This in itself may be bad (see below) and it's also the case that sedentary people tend to smoke more. In addition, obesity is associated with, and predisposes to, both hypertension and diabetes. But obesity *per se* in middle-aged men does not emerge as a powerful *independent* risk factor. That is, if you find a middle-aged fatty who does not smoke, has low blood cholesterol and is not hypertensive or diabetic, then he is only slightly more prone to heart attack than a middle-aged thinnie.

This does not mean, of course, that being fat in middle age is not dangerous. In fact losing weight may be the single most useful thing you can do, since many slimming diets can help to reduce your blood cholesterol and losing weight should reduce your blood pressure. I am pointing out the statistical niceties only because such niceties are part of the background debate.

Some factors are not heavily emphasised in most learned committee reports largely because they are too difficult to quantify. Thus few physicians would doubt, for example, that stress is an important contributor to heart attack. An increasing number are coming around to the view that, in practice, fostering a deep tranquillity may be one of the most useful things any individual could do. But nothing can be singled out as a risk factor unless (a) it can be measured, and (b) it can be correlated with the disease. And stress is notoriously difficult to measure. It certainly is not a simple thing that can be related to the concentration of some hormone in the blood, for example. Neither can we learn anything from any of the old-fashioned clichés about stress. It used to be suggested, for example, that CHD was an 'executive' disease, because executives suffered more stress. In fact, in modern Britain, heart disease seems to be commoner among the working classes, so that particular cliché is still-born.

One might also ask whether working class people *ever* had less stress than the middle classes, which on the face of it seems highly unlikely. In addition, there is no reason to suppose that people in poor countries, who commonly have less heart disease than those in rich countries, suffer any less stress. Indeed, it is now widely acknowledged that mental disturbance in general (of which, one assumes, stress is a significant component) is extremely common in Third World countries; certainly no rarer than in the west. In general, again, it is hard to see why anyone who is trying to make a living with the help of a water buffalo or half a dozen goats should be less stressed than the average European with a trade union and a state pension. Stress *must* be a factor in coronary heart disease, and anyone interested in long life should certainly seek peace of mind. But stress nonetheless seems to slip through the statistics, and 'risk factor' is a statistical concept.

Exercise is another of those tantalising ingredients of life which everyone knows must be important, but which again is difficult to pin down. Like stress, it is hard to measure. To take only one of many problems, how do you compare a once-weekly game of squash with a twice-daily stride to and from the office? There are indeed a few ingenious studies which overcome many of the difficulties, and which suggest that, in general, exercise is beneficial. Professor Jerry Morris at the London School of Hygiene and Tropical Medicine has shown that bus conductors get fewer heart attacks than drivers, and the main, consistent difference between them was that the conductors run up and down stairs all day. Exercise, in general, within reason, is a good thing.

Can risks be reduced?

Overall, then, we have a shortlist of important, independent risk factors; and a subsidiary list of other factors that are important but not independent, or which are probably important but are not easy to quantify. Can those risk factors be reduced and, if they can, will doing so lead to a longer life? In general, the answer to the first question at least is 'yes', though it's a 'yes' festooned with qualifying clauses.

Smoking is easily dealt with. Stop smoking and you cut out a major risk factor of CHD. Almost from the minute you stop, it seems, your risk goes down. Ex-smokers may be at no greater risk of heart attack than lifelong non-smokers. (They may of course already have sown the seeds of various chest diseases, but that is outside the brief of this book.)

Reducing dietary cholesterol is possible. It can be done by drugs, and it can be done by diet. Drugs certainly have a place in treatment, but few physicians these days would advocate mass use of drugs to lower blood cholesterol. The World Health Organisation ran a trial in which such a highly effective drug was used on large numbers of men. Their blood cholesterol did go down and so did the amount of coronary heart disease, so in that respect the trial was a success. But cholesterol is excreted in the bile, and when too much is excreted at once it tends to crystallise to form gallstones. Consequently, though heart disease went down, the incidence of liver disease increased and the overall mortality rate amongst these men was not affected.

The moral seems to be, therefore, that nature does not like to be rushed. However, a change in diet along the lines advocated above should reduce blood cholesterol naturally: cut down on fat and perhaps, where possible, substitute PUFAs for saturated fats (see pages 76–79).

Hypertension can also be reduced. If your doctor feels you need drugs to control your blood pressure, then he will give you drugs, and it is not for this book to comment on individual therapy. More generally, however, hypertension is often a result of being overweight: losing weight often brings down blood pressure, sometimes markedly. Some people, too, may reduce their blood pressure by going on a diet that is very low in salt, but we will discuss this subject further on page 124. It is also suggested that various specific methods of relaxation, including transcendental meditation, may reduce blood pressure. Again, this is outside the scope of this book.

The effects and importance of exercise are far from being well understood. Exhaustive treatment of what exercise may or may not do would require a book to itself at least as large as this one. But two points do seem relevant to our chosen theme of food and fats. One is that exercise undoubtedly has a part to play in the regulation of weight (which I will cover more fully in the chapter on obesity, on page 133). The other is that exercise evidently raises HDLs at the expense of LDLs. Even if total blood cholesterol is not reduced, therefore, the balance is tipped in your favour.

Healthy living, therefore, is as follows: modest, low-fat diet; no smoking; reasonable exercise. But if we turn ourselves into paragons, will it really do us any good?

CHD: cure or prevention?

Statistics are wonderful: they often reveal what is not obvious. They supplement everyday observation and reveal the limitations of unassisted common sense. But statistics, nonetheless, are just statistics. They are not prophecies. They deal only in probabilities.

Thus the best a statistician can say to you is that if you are the kind of person who (so statistics suggest) has a 10-to-one chance of having a heart attack in five years, then you might move yourself into the category of people who have only 100-to-one chance of a heart attack within five years. That is very far from a guarantee. One in 100 times, after all, the 100-to-one outsider wins: or, in this case, loses.

In addition, that is the *best* the statistician can say. For what is not yet entirely clear is whether, or to what extent, reducing risk factors late in life is as good as being free from those risk factors in the first place.

In practice, it seems that stopping smoking genuinely does increase chances of survival. Lowering blood pressure certainly reduces the chances of stroke (which itself is worth doing) and also, it seems, of heart attack. Whether or to what extent lowering blood cholesterol that has been high for some years increases your chances of survival is not at all clear. I can offer one encouraging comment and one discouraging one.

The encouraging observation is that there are countries in which the incidence of heart attack has gone down. Outstanding among these is the United States, in which the incidence of fatal coronary heart disease fell by an average of 3·6 per cent per year between 1968 and 1977. The United States has perhaps expended more total effort than any country in the world to exhort its people to mend their ways along the lines outlined in this book. In contrast, the incidence of fatal CHD rose by 1·1 per cent per year in England and Wales, and 0·5 per cent per year in Scotland, throughout the same period. In the UK, efforts to encourage the population to change its ways have come mainly from specific, small lobbies, which in general have enjoyed little 'official' support.

The discouraging comment is a common-sense observation, backed by very considerable clinical and statistical experience, by Britain's Dr Michael Oliver in Edinburgh. He points out that atheroma is a progressive disease. The arteries may be damaged over long periods, often over decades. There is very little evidence that atheroma regresses once established, or at least not to any significant degree. It's a little naïve, therefore, to assume that you cannot simply undo the evils of a lifetime by changing your ways in middle age, although the examples of the USA and Finland can give us hope.

But this is yet another of those points that we could go on arguing forever. Again, it's right and proper that scientists should go on arguing it in the hope of finally producing definitive advice. In the meantime, learned committees must make recommendations based on the best available evidence, flawed though that evidence may be; and all, in recent years, have recommended taking the kind of steps that seem to lead to a reduction of risk factors. That advice carries no cast-iron guarantees, but it does seem to make sense.

In the end, of course, individuals must make up their own minds. The best, perhaps, that we can ask from our guardians of health is that they should strive to make the issues as clear as possible. The sad thing is that in Britain at least there are many lobbies whose prime concern is to sell particular products; and to this end they tend to present highly selected facts and statistics that tend primarily to confuse. Thus, one of the least edifying public debates of recent years has been between the butter lobby and the purveyors of margarine. I don't want to libel anybody or dwell for too long on what is essentially a diversion; but a brief look at some of the arguments employed in the marge–butter conflict is called for.

Marge v. butter

It would take an entire book (and a fairly unsavoury one at that) to describe in full and lurid detail the attempts by the dairy lobby in Britain to do down the manufacturers of margarine, and vice versa. We, however, will stick to the points that pertain directly to nutrition.

There are three fronts on which the butter and marge protagonists can reasonably do battle. The first is flavour; but that's entirely for you to decide. The second is price; and that, of course, is clearly marked, so there is little scope for sleight of hand there. The third, which is our present concern, is health.

There are many minor chemical differences between butter and margarine but the one that seems to be of outstanding importance is the degree of saturation of the constituent fats. The point here (rightly made by the butter lobby) is that the vast majority of margarines contain as much, or almost as much, saturated fat as butter does. The only margarines significantly high in polyunsaturates are those made from highly unsaturated oils, notably sunflower and safflower. Those margarines that are made from these oils are clearly marked to that effect, and sometimes it is clearly stated that the margarine is indeed high in polyunsaturates. Those that are not so marked are made from all kinds of oils and fats, both vegetable and animal. Many vegetable oils, as we have seen, including the ubiquitous palm oil, are highly saturated, and many that begin by being unsaturated become saturated when they are 'hardened' to make margarine.

I have heard representatives of the dairy industry accuse the margarine lobby of bandwagoning – that is, of trying to sell all margarines on health grounds, whereas in fact only the small minority of polyunsaturated types can make a plausible claim to be less harmful than butter. The margarine manufacturers deny this, pointing out that the non-polyunsaturated margarines are sold not on the basis of healthfulness, but of price and flavour. I would not care to take sides in this; but the fact seems to be that many people wrongly believe that all margarine is in some way 'healthier' than butter, which means that a bandwagon effect has occurred even if it was not planned.

An issue of far less importance than the degree of saturation of the fats in butter or marge is the content of cholesterol. As I have mentioned, the Royal College of Physicians at least, in their eminently sensible report, did not feel that most people needed to worry too much about *dietary* cholesterol. The real issue is the amount of cholesterol *in the blood*, which is influenced by dietary fat in general; and dietary cholesterol is only a small component of overall dietary fat.

However, some margarines do carry a note to the effect that they are low in cholesterol, or contain none at all. This implies only that they are made mainly or exclusively from vegetable oil – which indeed contains no cholesterol. But vegetable oil in margarine is liable to be highly saturated unless otherwise stated. And, as we have seen, the degree of saturation of the fat is likely to be far more significant in dietary terms than the presence or absence of cholesterol. The Advertising Standards Authority in Britain demands that advertisements should not consciously deceive. Notes about cholesterol content seem to me to be highly deceptive, in that they imply a degree of healthfulness where none significantly exists. On the other hand the label 'high in polyunsaturates' does have real meaning for health-conscious consumers.

The calorie difference between butter and margarine is of no significance. Both are highly calorific. It makes sense, if you are trying to reduce your calorie intake, to cut down on fats in general; but it makes none at all to switch from butter to marge, or vice versa. Advertisements for butter have sometimes pointed out that margarine is as calorific as butter, and I am not quite sure whether this is done in the belief that some people think that margarine is less calorific (in which case it is perfectly legitimate to point out that this is not so) or is done in the spirit of disseminating red herrings: that is, implying that the health issue is about calories, whereas in fact it is about no such thing. In any case, comparison of calorie content is irrelevant.

There are of course low-calorie 'spreads' on the market, which may indeed pass as butter or marge and are in fact made from margarine with a very high content (around 50 per cent) of water. Whether there is any discernible difference between a watery 'spread' spread thickly, or a less watery spread spread thinly I regret is a matter I have not personally investigated. In general, however, low-calorie spreads seem to me to be an expensive way to buy water.

Neither side comes well out of the public squabble. The marge lobby, whatever its protests, does enjoy a bandwagon effect by cashing in on a growing, confused belief that margarine in general is better than butter in particular, which is dangerous nonsense. The butter lobby, for its part, has published a great deal that frankly is gobbledegook, not the least being the observation that butter gains from being 'natural'. How it can be natural for an adult primate (to whit *Homo sapiens*) to eat, in quantity, the fat extracted from the secretions of over-bred and over-fed bovines which were actually intended by nature to produce a rapid growth-rate in calves, is not at all clear.

The butter lobby has also strenuously sought to discredit the idea that saturated fats are harmful. This should not be dismissed out of hand. There must always be room for honest scepticism. I feel personally, however, (you must make up your own mind) that what they have presented is a rag-bag of arguments, which individually are not good, and which collectively add up to nothing coherent. For example, it has been publicly argued that the increase in heart disease in Britain during this century cannot possibly be related to an increase in fat intake, because Britons do not eat more fat now than they did at the turn of the century. Yet this cannot be true for most of the population. It is known that Britons used to eat a great deal more carbohydrate than they do now, and if they were also eating as much fat, then their daily energy intake must have been around 4000 kilocalories. This does not accord with the knowledge that many men were rejected for the Boer War and First World War because they were undernourished, or with the anecdotal evidence from many people (including one's own parents or grandparents) who lived through the early years of this century.

A second answer to this point is that the epidemiological case against saturated fat is not founded on historical evidence, but mainly on comparisons between present-day populations. The historical evidence (which in any case seems to me to be still intact) is merely a luxury.

We could pursue this. But marge v. butter could take over the book, and the main points have been made. The general advice is unequivocally to cut down on total fat intake and on saturated fat in particular. The extent to which you feel it is worthwhile launching a specific attack on dietary cholesterol or, at the present state of knowledge, moving over to polyunsaturated fats, must be your decision based on the kinds of arguments outlined above, and depending on which learned committee you find the most plausible. Information on particular foods about what contains what follows.

WHAT CAN WE DO ABOUT FAT?

Note:

Energy is measured in calories, and when comparing the different elements of food, nutritionists always talk about them in terms of their energy or calorie content in order to have a means of relating one element to another.

The NACNE report found that fat at present provides over 40% of the total energy in the British diet.

Reduce fat to 30%
of energy intake

In British terms this means reducing our fat intake by a quarter. How can we do this?

Look at Figure 5 on page 74, Where does the fat come from in the British diet? Although some foods have an appreciable fat content, e.g. mutton, the quantity of those foodstuffs actually consumed means that they only make up a small amount of our total fat intake. So for most people cutting out or down on these foods would make only a very marginal difference, although it might still be worthwhile substituting some foods for others (see Tables A, B and C). (Of course, if you don't eat an average 'British' diet then these foodstuffs may be more important to your overall fat intake than Figure 5 suggests.) But the most striking fact about the chart is the large amount of fat we eat which is derived from dairy sources – milk, cheese, butter (and its substitute, margarine) – and from sausages and other meat products. (Sausages and meat pies are often made from those parts of the animal carcass not easily sold as 'meat' so it is hardly surprising that their fat content is very high – up to 75% in some cheap sausages.)

If you want to follow the NACNE guidelines then it makes sense to look at the major sources of fat in your diet first. For example, if the average person switched from full fat milk (that's homogenised milk as well as the milk with a cream layer visible) to skimmed milk which has practically no fat, then immediately they would have reduced their fat intake by 14% which is well on the way to the 25% recommended. Even those who switched to semi-skimmed (which is like ordinary milk without the cream layer) would be saving, on average, 7% of their total fat intake. With this and a few other adjustments, it is not difficult to see that the NACNE guidelines are by no means revolutionary when it comes to reducing the amount of fat we consume.

But there is one other recommendation we need to consider:

Saturated fats should provide
no more than 10% of total
energy intake

At present the average Briton derives 17% of his total energy from saturated fats, so the NACNE guidelines do require a substantial reduction. So we should really start by looking at the sources of saturated fat in our diet.

Figure 6 shows that milk and butter are even more significant than Figure 5 indicates and that margarine is slightly less important. As we have seen in Chapter 5, this is not because *all* margarines have less saturated fat than butter, but because *some* are high in polyunsaturated fats. Therefore substitution of these polyunsaturated margarines for butter would reduce your total intake of saturated fats.

The following lists of foods showing their fat content will give you an idea of how to adjust your diet to meet the recommendations. However, it is not a good idea to concentrate your attention on this or that source of fat. Remember, the guidelines refer to the *percentage of energy* we derive from fat, so if we increase our intake of non-fatty foods – bread and potatoes in particular – our intake of fat-derived calories should automatically decrease. Most people will eat the same amount of calories in total, so the actual as well as percentage amount of fat would decrease. As we will see in the next chapter, there are other good reasons for increasing our consumption of carbohydrates quite apart from the advantage of reducing fat.

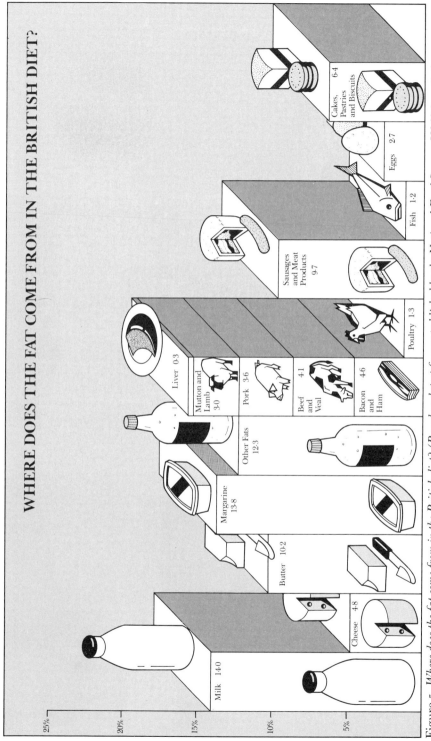

WHERE DOES THE FAT COME FROM IN THE BRITISH DIET?

Milk 14·0

Cheese 4·8

Butter 10·2

Margarine 13·8

Other Fats 12·3

Liver 0·3

Mutton and Lamb 3·0

Pork 3·6

Beef and Veal 4·1

Bacon and Ham 4·6

Poultry 1·3

Sausages and Meat Products 9·7

Fish 1·2

Eggs 2·7

Cakes, Pastries and Biscuits 6·4

Figure 5 *Where does the fat come from in the British diet? (Based on latest figures published by the National Food Survey, HMSO, 1984.)*

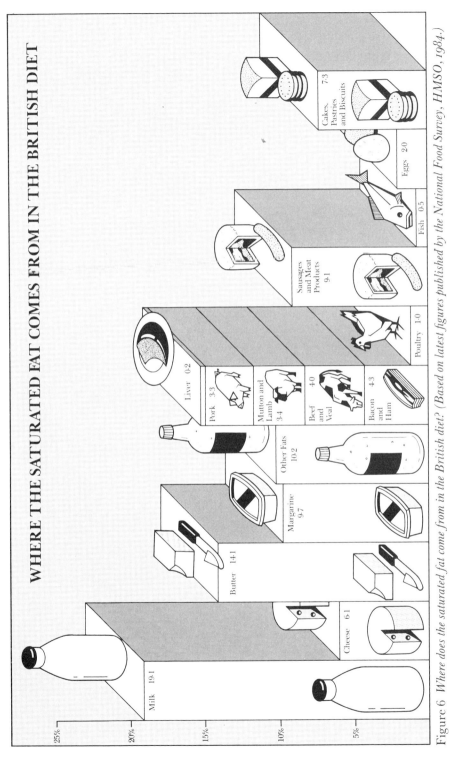

WHERE THE SATURATED FAT COMES FROM IN THE BRITISH DIET

Milk 19·1
Butter 14·1
Margarine 9·7
Other Fats 10·2
Liver 0·2
Pork 3·3
Mutton and Lamb 3·4
Beef and Veal 4·0
Bacon and Ham 4·3
Poultry 1·0
Sausages and Meat Products 9·1
Fish 0·5
Eggs 2·0
Cakes, Pastries and Biscuits 7·3
Cheese 6·1

25%
20%
15%
10%
5%

Figure 6 *Where does the saturated fat come from in the British diet? (Based on latest figures published by the National Food Survey, HMSO, 1984.)*

TABLE A

FOODS CONTAINING SATURATED FAT

To reduce the number of calories you derive from saturated fat in your diet, try eating fewer of the foods in Columns A and B and substituting as many as you can from Column C.

A	B	C
Foods providing a lot of calories from saturated fat	**Foods providing some calories from saturated fat**	**Foods providing very few calories from saturated fat**
Butter	Polyunsaturated margarines	Chicken, roast, without skin
Cream	Sunflower oil	Turkey, roast, without skin
Lard	Corn oil	Kidneys
Palm oil	Soya oil	Haddock
Unspecified vegetable oil	Ice-cream	Cod
Hard margarine	Cottage cheese	Plaice
Cheese, e.g.	Semi-skimmed milk	Smoked salmon
Stilton	Eggs	Shellfish, e.g.
Cheddar	Lean meat, e.g.	
Camembert	beef	prawns
Edam	leg lamb	mussels
Gold top milk	leg pork	cockles
Silver top milk	pork chop	Skimmed milk
Fatty meat, e.g.	Chicken, roast, with skin	Low-fat yoghurt
shoulder lamb	Rabbit	Wholemeal bread
belly pork	Ham	Muesli
lamb chop	Liver, grilled	Breakfast cereal
Corned beef	Herrings	Jacket potatoes
Luncheon meat	Mackerel	Sweet potatoes
Pork sausages	Tinned salmon	Rice
Frankfurters	Tinned sardines	Pasta
Salami	Tinned tuna	Walnuts
Bacon, grilled and fried	Peanuts	Matzos
Coconut	Peanut butter	Crispbread
Chocolate biscuits	Sponge cake	Most fruit
Chocolate digestive biscuits	Semi-sweet biscuits	Salad vegetables
Sandwich biscuits	Avocado pears	Root vegetables

TABLE B

TYPES OF FAT IN DIFFERENT FOODS IN DESCENDING ORDER OF SATURATED FAT CONTENT

Food	Saturated	Mono-unsaturated	Poly-unsaturated
Cream, double	58	31	3
Cream, single	54	29	2
Stilton cheese	46	25	2
Cheddar cheese	44	24	2
Cheese, Camembert type	41	22	2
Edam cheese	40	22	2
Lamb, shoulder, roast, lean and fat	37	28	3
Salami	33	37	6
Frankfurters	33	37	6
Fresh milk, whole	31	17	2
Pork belly, grilled, lean and fat	31	35	6
Luncheon meat	29	36	7
Pork sausage, grilled	27	33	6
Shortbread	27	15	2
Sandwich biscuits	25	14	3
Flaky pastry	25	27	8
Bacon, fried, lean only	24	27	4
Bacon, grilled, lean only	24	26	4
Ice cream, dairy	23	9	1
Digestive biscuits	23	17	3
Ice cream, non-dairy	23	16	3
Cottage cheese	22	12	1
Short-crust pastry	22	23	7
Corned beef	21	24	2
Duck, roast, with skin	21	41	9
Eggs	21	26	7
Chicken, roast, with skin	19	26	9
Choux pastry	19	23	8
Sponge cake	19	22	7
Lamb, leg, roast, lean only	19	14	2
Mackerel	16	25	16
Rabbit, stewed	16	8	12
Semi-sweet biscuits	16	12	3
Peanut butter	15	39	19
Salmon, steamed	15	23	15
Fruit cake, plain	15	13	3
Peanuts	15	37	22
Ham	14	17	4
Olives in brine	13	67	11

Pork, leg, roast, lean only	13	15	3
Liver, chicken	13	9	8
Liver, calf's	13	7	11
Pheasant	13	19	5
Duck, roast, without skin	13	25	6
Tuna, tinned	12	27	25
Salmon, tinned	12	18	12
Herring, grilled	12	30	10
Sardines, tinned	11	31	11
Chicken, roast, without skin	11	15	5
Beef, topside, lean only	11	12	1
Avocado pear	11	67	8
Yoghurt, low-fat natural	10	5	0
Walnuts	10	14	0
Kidney, lamb's	9	6	4
Salmon, smoked	7	11	7
Almonds	7	58	6
Turkey, roast, without skin	6	4	6
Kidney, pig's	4	7	4
Crab, boiled	4	7	4
Mussels, boiled	4	4	6
Oysters	4	2	5
Muesli	3	7	7
Halibut, steamed	3	6	9
Lobster, boiled	3	5	9
Plaice, steamed	3	5	4
Porridge	3	7	7
Peas, boiled	3	2	Less than 1
Cod's roe, hard	3	3	4
Bread, wholemeal	2	2	5
Cod, baked	2	1	4
Spinach	2	1	9
Prawns, boiled	2	3	6
Bread, white	2	1	3
Weetabix	1	1	4
Haddock, steamed	1	1	2
Shredded Wheat	1	1	3
Fresh milk, skimmed	1	1	Nil
Runner beans, boiled	1	Nil	3
Flour, wholemeal	Less than 1	Less than 1	3
Macaroni	Less than 1	Less than 1	2
Cornflakes	Less than 1	1	2
Rice	Less than 1	Less than 1	Less than 1
Spaghetti	Less than 1	Negligible	1
Potatoes, old, boiled	Negligible	Nil	Less than 1

TABLE C

TYPES OF FAT IN DIFFERENT KINDS OF OILS AND FATS IN DESCENDING ORDER OF SATURATED FAT

Food	Saturated	Mono-unsaturated	Poly-unsaturated
Coconut oil	85	7	2
Butter	60	32	3
Palm oil	45	42	8
Lard	43	42	9
Beef dripping	40	49	4
Margarine, hard (vegetable only)	37	47	12
Margarine, hard (mixed oils)	37	43	17
Margarine, soft (vegetable)	32	42	22
Margarine, soft (mixed oils)	30	45	19
Low fat spread	27	38	30
Margarine, polyunsaturated	24	20	74
Ground nut oil	19	48	28
Maize oil	16	29	49
Wheat germ oil	14	11	45
Soya bean oil	14	24	57
Olive oil	14	70	11
Sunflower seed oil	13	32	50
Safflower seed oil	10	13	72
Rape seed oil	7	64	32

Chapter 6

CARBOHYDRATE REVISITED

Carbohydrates, like proteins and fats, are an astonishingly varied group of compounds. Table sugar is carbohydrate; starch is carbohydrate; cotton, kapok and gum are carbohydrate. There are carbohydrates both in plant tissue and in animal tissue; animals, indeed, store a fair amount in the form of glycogen. Babies obtain all the carbohydrate they need from animal sources – from lactose, the unique sugar of milk. But after weaning, most human beings derive by far the majority of their carbohydrate from plant sources, and in this chapter (as is the case in most texts on nutrition) when I speak of carbohydrate I mean 'plant carbohydrate', and when I speak of a high carbohydrate diet I mean one that contains a lot of plant material.

All carbohydrates consist of sugars, or things very like sugars, or materials compounded of sugars – that is, polymers of sugars. There are scores of different sugars and many thousands of ways of arranging different sugars in chains and of branching those chains. In practice, each species of plant tends to make the various polymers in its own individual way, and so there is, if not an infinity, then at least an astronomical number of different carbohydrates in nature. But we can place those carbohydrates, conveniently, into four main classes.

First, there are the sugars themselves. There are many different kinds, and many of them feature from time to time in discussions on nutrition. But three are of overwhelming significance. The first of these is glucose – a simple, six-carbon sugar, which is the commonest organic molecule in nature. Then there is fructose, also a six-carbon sugar (but different, nonetheless, from glucose) which is found, characteristically, in fruit: the 'fruct' implies fruit, as in 'fructify'. And then there is the sugar that plays such an enormous part in the western diet and probably has profound effects on human health: sucrose, which appears on every tea-table and in most processed foods, and is eaten by the million ton. Sucrose is a disaccharide: that is, it is compounded of two sugar molecules – specifically, one glucose joined to one fructose.

In the second category is starch. Starch is the principal form in which plants store carbohydrate for food energy. Starches are variable just as all natural polymers are variable: but all starch consists essentially of molecules of glucose joined together.

Plants produce sugars and starch to provide themselves with energy, and we simply expropriate, or steal, what they have produced. As sugars and starch are intended as energy it is hardly surprising that they are readily digestible and absorbable; and, indeed, the gut easily absorbs the simple sugars, glucose and fructose, and produces enzymes which break sucrose and starch into its constituent simple sugars, which it then absorbs.

But plants also employ carbohydrates to make their skeletons – the thick walls with which they surround each and every cell, and which enable them to stand upright. These skeletal cell walls are not intended to be broken down to be used to supply energy. Indeed they are intended to resist breakdown and to stand as long as the plant stands, which, in the case of some desert pines, may be thousands of years. Not surprisingly, then, the gut does not cope with these cell-wall carbohydrates anything like so summarily as with sugars and starch. Consequently, in the old days of nutrition, these structural carbohydrates were called 'unavailable carbohydrate', or, more perfunctorily, 'roughage'. We will see later in this chapter that both those terms in practice are inappropriate, and nutritionists now prefer the expression 'dietary fibre'. All will become clear, but for the moment let us complete our list, and observe that dietary fibre contains our two remaining categories of carbohydrate as follows.

The third class of carbohydrates includes the hemicelluloses and pectins. The chemistry of these compounds is horrendously complicated: they include many peculiar kinds of sugar and obscure sugar-like compounds, and they vary markedly in chemistry from species to species. We may leave the details to the polymer chemists. Suffice to observe that the hemicelluloses and pectins form a significant part of plant cell walls; indeed, in any one cell wall they may be the major components. In addition, although the details are not well understood, it's clear that the chemistry of the particular hemicelluloses and pectins found in any one kind of fibre profoundly influences the effect that that fibre has on the human gut. Thus, later in this chapter we will see that nutritionists may recommend different kinds of fibre in different contexts. But this is not mumbo-jumbo: different kinds of fibre from different plants are profoundly different entities, and the difference depends, in large part, on the hemicelluloses and pectins.

The final category of carbohydrate includes the commonest polymer in nature: cellulose. Cellulose, like starch, is compounded exclusively of glucose. But unlike starch it is not intended to be digested for use as food. Thus, the glucose molecules in starch are arranged in such a way that digestive enzymes can gain easy access: but in cellulose they are arranged in wire-like strands, which are bound together in the cell walls by the hemicelluloses and pectins. No animal has ever been shown unequivocally to produce an enzyme that can digest cellulose. But many bacteria can digest this form of carbohydrate, and herbivorous animals commonly, or indeed usually, harbour colonies of such bacteria in their guts to digest it for them. Ruminant animals, such as cows, store such bacteria in a huge fermenting chamber known as the rumen, which forms part of their stomach. These bacteria digest the cellulose, although they do not simply digest it cleanly into its constituent sugars; they instead break it into smaller molecules, known as volatile fatty acids, or VFAS. I mention this only because it is (as we will see) slightly relevant to human beings; but the main thing to observe here is that for cows, but decidedly not for humans, cellulose is the principal source of energy.

Cellulose is remarkably tough stuff. It is the compound of which cotton is made. And when the cellulose molecules are buckled together by small amounts of lignin (which is not a carbohydrate) it becomes wood, one of the most miraculously powerful materials in nature (until, that is, it is digested away by fungi, and collapses in a mouldering heap).

But let us return to the nutrition of human beings and ask what effect these various classes of carbohydrate have upon us.

Refined and unrefined

In the bad old days of nutritional science (which, in this context, means before the late 1970s) few nutritionists had anything interesting to say about carbohydrates. In general, they considered that starch and sugar were reasonable, and certainly cheap, sources of energy, and to that extent desirable; but they warned against eating too much 'starchy food' because that, they suggested, would lead to obesity. The 'unavailable' forms of carbohydrate were effectively written off. They were called 'roughage', and the only beneficial thing that roughage could be shown unequivocally to do was to ease constipation. On the other hand (though the topic has waxed and waned), constipation has tended widely to be disregarded in recent years, so even this small stronghold of 'roughage' was under siege. The overall tone of nutritional advice throughout the 1950s and 1960s was that food, in general, should be stripped of indigestible appurtenance. The ideal diet to which we all seemed to be moving, and which was recommended for those countries that were still 'developing', was one packed with nutriment in every molecule: high in protein, high (if only by default) in the energy provided by fat and sugar, and heavily laced with vitamins. It was a no-nonsense approach to nutrition, which saw the human body merely as a machine like any other, which needed energy to run; and since machines liked their energy as pure as possible, their fuels fractionated and distilled to provide only what could be burned most efficiently, why not the human body? To think otherwise was to be a muddle-headed romantic.

Throughout the 1960s a number of doctors began to question that received and polished wisdom. It's important and interesting that they were doctors: clinicians, both physicians and surgeons, whose knowledge of the human condition came not merely from theorising (although they were excellent theorists) but from first-hand knowledge of the real patients. Outstanding among these pioneers (as I am sure those not here listed will agree) were Surgeon Captain T L Cleave; Dr Denis Burkitt; and Dr Hugh Trowell.

Dr Cleave, together with Dr G D Campbell, a physician, and Mr Neil Painter, a surgeon, set the tone in 1966 with their revelationary volume, *Diabetes, Coronary Thrombosis, and the Saccharine Disease* (John Wright & Sons, Bristol). Dr Cleave followed this up with his own book, *The Saccharine Disease*, in 1974.

The term 'saccharine' in those titles is an adjective meaning 'relating to sugars and sugar-like substances', and the last syllable rhymes with 'pine'. It does not allude to the synthetic sweetener (in which the '-ine' rhymes with 'pin'). The burden of the two books is that the conditions known as the 'diseases of affluence' result largely from our abandonment of a diet that was high in natural, unadulterated plants – high, that is, in 'unrefined' carbohydrate – for one that contained large amounts of 'refined' carbohydrate, which principally meant sugar and white flour. The list of diseases of affluence grew as the protagonists warmed to the theme, and came to include coronary heart disease, diabetes, gallstones, obesity, and various conditions of the large intestine ranging from constipation to diverticular disease and cancer of the colon.

Dr Richard Doll (now Sir Richard Doll, who discovered the link between smoking and lung cancer), wrote the foreword to *Diabetes, Coronary Thrombosis, and the Saccharine Disease*. He said: 'Whether the predictions . . . in this book will prove to be correct remains to be seen; but if only a small part of them do, the authors will have made a bigger contribution to medicine than most university departments or medical research units make in the course of a generation.'

It's nearly 20 years since Sir Richard wrote that; and now the point is largely vindicated. There is extensive evidence that the amount of carbohydrate we eat – and, more importantly, the form in which we eat it – has a great influence upon all the diseases of affluence. The outstanding conceptual advance since Dr Cleave's work of 1966 is by Hugh Trowell, who simply pointed out that the principal, tangible difference between refined and unrefined carbohydrate was that the latter contained all the original cell walls. In other words, it contained 'dietary fibre', a term that seems to have been with us forever but in fact was first coined in print, by Dr Trowell, in 1972.

In short, modern nutritional theory now revolves around carbohydrate; and the crucial point, as Dr Cleave enunciated right at the beginning, is to distinguish between *refined* carbohydrate, and *unrefined*. In general, just to set the scene, modern nutritionists tend to argue that the human diet should contain a great deal of carbohydrate. Indeed, if we believe the American McGovern report, which suggested that we should obtain only 30 per cent of our calories from fat, or the British Royal College of Physicians, who put the figure at 35 per cent; and if we accept that (in round figures) 12 to 15 per cent of our diet should consist of protein; then we see that we are being invited to obtain at least 50 per cent of our daily calories from carbohydrate.

But – and this 'but' should be written six feet high – this carbohydrate should be *unrefined*. It should be eaten as nearly as possible in the state in which the plant first produced it. Just to labour the point, the old-fashioned advice to avoid too much sugar and starch remains more or less intact; but what we are now being urged to do is to eat large amounts not of extracted plant products, but of *plants*.

Before we explore the merits of unrefined carbohydrate in general, and of dietary fibre in particular, we should look briefly first at refined carbohydrates, both what the term actually implies and at some of the drawbacks.

Refined and unrefined, the meaning of the terms

The words 'refined' and 'unrefined' unfortunately tend to be used in slightly different contexts, and thus at different times to have different connotations. They also tend, from time to time, to be jumbled up with words such as 'natural' and 'unnatural'. Worse, there are people in this world who exploit confusion and set out to deceive. A brief note is called for, then, just to talk around the terms.

Refined carbohydrates are edible, easily digested carbohydrates that have been removed from the plant that first produced them. Point one, perhaps, is that some of the processes by which these digestible carbohydrates are extracted are 'natural', in the sense that they are performed by agents other than human; and some are 'unnatural', in the sense that they are carried out exclusively by human beings. Chief by far of the 'natural' sources of refined carbohydrate is honey, which is sugar taken from plants and concentrated by bees. Natural it is, but in nature it is rare (comparatively speaking) and is guarded by possessive creatures. The fact that it is a natural product does not save it from the opprobrium that must attach to all refined carbohydrate.

Nutritionally, honey is not superior to sugar, molasses, treacle, syrup, or any other concentrated sugar that human beings, most unnaturally, extract from grasses (sugar cane) and roots (sugar beet). I believe that honey has two saving graces, but neither has to do with nutritional theory. The first is that it tastes nice and can be used in small quantities as a 'spice'; and the second is that it is expensive, so you would not be tempted (as with sugar) to float entire meals in it. I examined the term 'natural' in Chapter 2 and I hope that from that chapter you caught the message 'Beware!'.

Point two is that there are degrees of refinement. The pure white crystals of sugar that have graced a billion tea-tables are refined as refinedly as technology can achieve. The manufacturer would be affronted, if not litigious, if you suggested that his crystals contained fibre. To him, this would imply incompetence, if not adulteration.

But brown sugar, particularly the lumpy kind, is sometimes sold as 'unrefined' sugar. There is no doubt a technical justification for using this term but it does not mean unrefined in the sense that nutritionists mean unrefined. The sugar, pure sucrose, has been extracted from the original plant just as assiduously as the white kind. Unrefined it may be by the standards of industrial chemists, but in botanical terms, or in nutritional terms, it is as pure, as refined, as driven snow.

White flour, and the white bread made from it, are also commonly categorised as 'refined' carbohydrate. Dr Cleave himself, indeed, categorised them in just this way. I would not presume to argue: for the purposes of this discussion it is indeed best to regard white flour as refined because the starch it contains is rapidly and easily digested and absorbed, and hence has much the same immediate effect on the physiology as a draught of glucose syrup might do. However, I think it should be pointed out that there are important differences between refined white flour and refined sugar.

For one thing, white flour does contain some fibre. The samples of self-raising that Drs Alison Paul and David Southgate analysed for their revision of the classic *The Composition of Foods* (HMSO, London, 1976) contained 3·7 per cent by weight. Admittedly, their samples of wholemeal flour contained 9·6 per cent fibre. But my point is not so much to emphasise that white flour contains fibre, but to warn that it belongs, because of its physiological effects, in the category of refined carbohydrate *despite* containing an appreciable amount of fibre.

White flour, as eaten in Britain, is '70 per cent extract'. That is, 30 per cent of the original wheat grain has been removed including the embryo of the wheat (the 'germ') and most of the fibrous outer layers, which constitute the 'bran'. Wholemeal is, of course, 100 per cent extract: germ, bran, and all. However, in our condemnation of white flour I am not at all convinced that we should leap too athletically towards wholemeal, wholemeal, and nothing but wholemeal. In many parts of the world – most, indeed, outside the modern technological influence – flour is refined up to a point; enough to produce extracts between, say, the upper 70s and upper 80s. The dough from such flours produces cream-coloured loaves (or pitta, or whatever) that lack the heroic quality sometimes associated with wholemeal bread, but nonetheless have a respectable 6–7 per cent content of fibre. The bread of southern Italy (it isn't all pasta in those parts) is one of the delights of human existence; and diets based upon such bread would not, one feels, be outside the modern nutritional pale. This is, in short, a modest plea for compromise.

The second point is that white flour does not *only* contain carbohydrate. In this respect it is profoundly different, nutritionally, from sugar. Indeed white flour has a perfectly respectable protein content (around 9·5 per cent). This point has, of course, nothing whatever to do with our discussion of fibre, but it is pertinent to the whole question of whether human beings can safely be recommended to eat large amounts of plant food; and the answer is, just for reassurance, that they can, provided the plant food is in the form of seeds such as cereal (which can be milled to produce flour). The issue is discussed more fully on page 93, and I mention it here only to make the point that just because white flour and sugar can for some purposes be placed in the same category (that is, they can both be classed as refined carbohydrate), this does not mean that they are nutritionally identical, or equivalent. It's important not to get carried away by classification.

To understand why modern nutritionists are so round in their condemnation of refined carbohydrates, we must pursue two lines of argument: first, discuss (briefly) some of the specific demerits of refined carbohydrates, and then (more extensively) outline some of the advantages of unrefined carbohydrates.

The drawbacks of refined carbohydrates – particularly sugar

From all the long and intricate literature on unrefined carbohydrates, and sugar in particular, we can pick out two clear and recurrent themes. The first is that sugar is the principal, and in modern society virtually the only, begetter of dental caries. And the second is that refined carbohydrates in general, but sugar in particular, slip down the throat, and into the blood stream all too easily. We will discuss this second aspect later, within the contexts of obesity and of diabetes. But first, to begin at the top, teeth.

Sugar and caries

It isn't true, as is sometimes suggested, that our ancient ancestors suffered no caries at all. But they had very little, and what they had didn't occur in the same place as it does today and did not occur until late in life.

Thus the teeth in the skulls of ancient Romans and Egyptians tended to be beautifully free from blemish for the first couple of decades or so of life. But the food in those days, at least for common people, was not only egregiously fibrous (and compared to which the modern wholemeal loaf is positively effete), but was also filled with mineral, not least from the stones with which they ground their flour. Hence, as the third decade of life gave way to the fourth (the fifth was a luxury that few attained) the teeth became flatter and flatter. Such was their shape – they were narrow at the base – that as they became flatter, so spaces opened between them. Within these spaces, caries appeared, although by modern standards very little. Caries may, however, have been the least of their worries. Greater was the effect of wear itself, exposing the nerves and leading to appalling abscesses, which are indicated in the remaining skulls by perforations around the maxillae.

Such was the pattern, with greater or less flattening of teeth, throughout Saxon times. But the skulls that lie in the plague pits of England, dating from 1665, show a little more caries. By the end of the seventeenth century, after all, the average English person was consuming 10 lb of sugar per year.

The modern pattern begins in the nineteenth century, as has been splendidly illustrated by Professor James Moore of Leeds University. He studied skulls from two graveyards at Ashton-under-Lyne, which is now a district of Manchester. One of those graveyards, attached to the church of St Michael and All Angels, contains graves from before 1850. The other, at Stanford Street, is post-1850 and designed to accommodate a population that swelled, typically and dramatically, from 15,000 to 86,000 during the industrial years of the nineteenth century.

The pre-1850 skulls in St Michael and All Angels show much the same level of caries as those from the 17th-century plague pits. Those of Stanford Street have practically reached the modern level of decay. The position of the caries changed too: no longer does it appear between the teeth, but on their grinding surfaces. It was in the middle of the nineteenth century, from 1845 to 1875, that the duty on sugar, which at that time was all imported, was steadily reduced and finally abolished, so that by the end of the that century consumption had reached 90 lb per year.

This is anecdote: not proof, nor intended as such. But the evidence now is so overwhelming that we need do no more than indulge in illustration. Sugar nourishes bacteria in the mouth. Those bacteria produce acid, which dissolves tooth enamel. Enamel can be, and is constantly restored: it is not laid down once and for all and then abandoned to its fate, as once was thought. Sugar eaten as an occasional spice (with plenty of time between each session) should give the teeth time to recover. But the modern diet offers no respite.

Sugar and obesity

In the bad old days, before the sharp distinction was drawn between refined carbohydrate and unrefined, nutritionists seemed fairly broadly agreed that carbohydrate, in general, predisposed to obesity. Now that the distinction has been well and truly made, the lore is quite different. Now we can say, without fear of much contradiction, that sugar in particular, the most refined carbohydrate of them all, is a major contributor to obesity. We can also say, although the point is more complicated, that diets in which most of the energy is provided by unrefined carbohydrate help people to reach or maintain their ideal body weight. But let us first look a little longer at sugar.

The reason that sugar contributes so significantly to obesity is that people eat a great deal of it. That might sound obvious, and indeed banal, but in fact it is remarkable. We are able to eat so much only because sugar combines several different and unrelated qualities.

First of all, of course, it tastes nice: sugar is a highly prized spice, with the power to become addictive. Secondly, and quite unrelatedly, it attracts water and thus, when put into food, denies water to invading bacteria. Hence it is an excellent preservative. Thirdly, sugar is highly soluble and so easily taken in liquid form: but at the same time, when in highly concentrated solution, it can contribute much to the texture of food, producing smooth and pleasant viscosity. Finally, it is cheap.

Thus, sugar is used in many foods and in many contexts; and, above all, it is the food processors' delight, offering tastiness, shelf-life and texture in one swoop, and at little cost. Even foods that are ostensibly savoury contain sugar as an important if not the principal ingredient. Tomato ketchup often contains more than 20 per cent sugar and so too does brown sauce. Sweet pickle may be 30 per cent sugar and chutney 50 per cent. More obviously, perhaps, marmalade is likely to contain nearly 70 per cent sugar plus 28 per cent water (anything called jam or marmalade has to contain 60 per cent sugar by law). Sugar is not the most calorific of foods (gram for gram, fat provides twice as much energy) but it nonetheless provides more than 4 kcal to the gram, which is 1800 or so to the pound. Given that sugar appears in such quantity in so many foods, it's hardly surprising that Britons, on average, obtain nearly a fifth of their daily calories from sugar – and as that is an average, many people must obtain far more than that.

If human beings simply adjusted their intake of food to their energy requirements, then, of course, sugar would be no more fattening than anything else. We would simply consume enough to keep us at our ideal weight, and then stop – whether we were eating sugar, or anything else. But in practice energy requirement is only one of several factors that determine the amount we actually eat. Palatability has a great influence – and sugar is highly palatable. Ease of consumption has an influence, as we will explore in slightly more detail in the next section, and sugar slips straight down, especially when taken in solution, as a drink. In short, it seems designed to make people fat. Putting the point the other way, if we continue to derive 400 or so kcal from sugar every day, it is hard to see how most of us can ever expect to be slim.

HOW MUCH SUGAR ARE YOU EATING?

Apart from the sugar you consciously add to drinks or food, sugar is also contained in many manufactured foods. Approximately 60% of the sugar consumed in the UK is taken in this way.

Reduce sucrose consumption
to 20kg per head per year

NACNE RECOMMENDATIONS

This recommendation is based on the amount of sugar available for consumption in the UK. Allowing for a certain percentage of wastage that is inevitable, this can be translated into the maximum number of teaspoons recommended per day per person.

An ideal diet would contain no sucrose, but the maximum to meet the recommendations should not be greater than 10 teaspoons per day from any source.

See how you fare from the table overleaf.
If the precise food you eat is not included, take the nearest approximation.

NB: The sugar content of these foods may vary but this is a reasonable guide.

HOW MUCH SUGAR IS IN THE FOODS YOU EAT?

Have a look at the list below and check. The recommendation is not more than a total of 10 teaspoons a day (including all those added to tea and coffee.) If you can take less, so much the better.

Food	Amount	Number of teaspoons of sugar
Biscuits		
Bran biscuit	1 biscuit	3
Chocolate digestive	½ biscuit	1
Digestive	1 biscuit	½
Ginger nuts	1 biscuit	1
Plain biscuits		
e.g. Marie, Rich Tea	2 biscuits	½
Drinks		
Apeel Orange Drink	1 small glass	2
Bitter lemon	1 med. bottle	5
Blackcurrant cordial	1 glass	6
Cola	1 can	7
Ginger ale	1 med. bottle	4
Lemonade	1 glass	2
Lucozade	1 glass	7
Orange/Lemon squash	1 glass	2
Ribena	1 glass	6
Tonic water	1 med. bottle	2
Vimto	1 glass	3
Spreads		
Chocolate spread	2 teaspoons	2
Honey, Jam, Marmalade	2 teaspoons	2
Lemon curd	2 teaspoons	2
Breakfast Cereals		
Allbran	1 bowl	1
Bran Buds	1 bowl	1½
Bran Flakes	1 bowl	1½
Coco Pops	1 bowl	3
Muesli	2 tablespoons	1–2
Shredded Wheat	1 biscuit	0
Shreddies	1 bowl	½
Sugar Frosties	1 bowl	3½
Sugar Puffs	1 bowl	3
Sugar Smacks	1 bowl	½
Sultana bran	1 bowl	1
Weetabix	1 biscuit	¼

Food	Amount	Number of teaspoons of sugar
Cakes		
Chocolate cake	1 med. slice	2
Chocolate cake & icing	1 med. slice	5
Currant bun	1 bun	1
Doughnut	1 bun	1½
Fruit cake	1 med. slice	3
Fruit pie	1 med. slice	2
Jam tart	1 med. slice	3
Madeira cake	1 med. slice	2
Sponge cake	1 med. slice	1½
Sponge sandwich	1 med. slice	4½
Desserts		
Creme caramel	2 tablespoons	2
Chocolate mousse	2 tablespoons	3
Chocolate sauce	3 tablespoons	6
Dream topping	1 sachet	2
Fresh fruit cream dessert	1 small carton	3
Fruit-flavoured yoghurt	1 small carton	3
Fruit yoghurt	1 small carton	3
Ice cream	small block	9
Instant custard	1 pkt.	7
Instant whip	1 pkt.	10
Jelly	1 pkt.	19
Sponge pudding with jam/syrup	1 med. slice	5
Tinned fruit	1 small tin	5
Tinned rice pudding	½ tin	2½
Trifle	2 tablespoons	2
Water ice	2 tablespoons	2
Beverages		
Bournvita	3 teaspoons	1½
Drinking chocolate	3 teaspoons	2
Horlicks	3 teaspoons	2
Ovaltine	3 teaspoons	2
Sauces, Pickles etc.		
Brown sauce	3 teaspoons	1
Mango chutney	3 teaspoons	1
Sweet pickle	3 teaspoons	1
Tomato chutney	3 teaspoons	1

Food	Amount	Number of teaspoons of sugar
Soups		
Packet oxtail	¼ pkt.	1
Packet tomato	¼ pkt.	2
Tinned tomato	½ tin	1
Tinned vegetable	½ tin	1
Tinned vegetables		
Baked beans	½ med. tin	2
Kidney beans	1 small tin	1½
Sweet corn	⅓ med. tin	1½
Confectionery		
Aero	1 bar	3½
Banjo	2 biscuit	3
Boiled sweets	1 tube	10
Bounty	2 pieces	4
Cabana	1 bar	6
Caramel	1 bar	5½
Chocolate, milk	1 small bar	6½
Chocolate, fruit/nut	1 bar	4
Chocolate, whole nut	1 bar	4
Chocolate, plain	1 small bar	6
Chocolate cream	1 bar	7
Crunchie	1 bar	6
Dolly Mixtures	1 small box	20½
Double Decker	1 bar	6
Drifter	1 pkt.	6½
Fruit Gums	1 tube	3
Galaxy	1 bar	4
Kit Kat	1 bar	4
Liquorice Allsorts	1 small box	18
Lion Bar	1 bar	5½
Marathon	1 bar	3½
Maltesers	1 pkt.	2½
Mars	1 bar	9
Milky Way	1 bar	1½
Murray Mints	1 pkt.	10
Picnic	1 bar	5
Polo Mints	1 tube	5
Rolo	1 tube	5½

The advantages of unrefined carbohydrate – the role of fibre

Sugar, then, most refined of carbohydrates, is an important cause of obesity. On the other hand, Dr Cleave and Dr Trowell in particular have argued that diets that are very high in unrefined carbohydrate prevent obesity. Dr Trowell points out that obesity is unknown among, for example, African villagers, who obtain 70 per cent or more of their calories from unrefined carbohydrates. But what makes the difference? How is it that carbohydrates in one form are fattening, while ostensibly the same materials in another form are not?

The obvious point, of course, is that a diet high in unrefined carbohydrate inevitably contains a great deal of fibre. But this point, taken by itself, can be highly deceptive. What it emphatically does not mean is that fibre, as fibre, will stop you getting fat. In hotels, where I occasionally get to stay, I have seen businessmen of my own age tucking in to the All-bran, which indeed is marvellously high in fibre (nearly 27 per cent by weight); but they follow it up with egg, bacon, sausage, toast, butter and marmalade, and coffee which they austerely leave black and perversely spike with sugar. Thus they have a diet high in fibre, but high, also, in fat and sugar, and hence in calories. The bran in the All-bran doubtless stirs their bowels, and if that is the limit of their ambition, then fair enough. But a high calorie diet is a high calorie diet, whether wrapped around fibre or not.

There are many variations on this theme, from the huge and pleasant salads served in many areas of the United States piled high with blue-cheese dressing or mayonnaise; to the high-cereal, high-vegetable (and hence high-fibre) offerings of the average Indian takeaway which also, to please the western palate, tend to be soaked in butter. The role of fibre in slimming is not to act as a panacea – as a drug to be added to the same type of food as usual.

The point is, of course, that when Cleave and Trowell speak of high-fibre diets they mean *diets in which the major proportion of the energy comes from unrefined carbohydrate*, and which, consequently, are low in fat and low in unrefined carbohydrate. It's simply a matter of arithmetic. If, like an African villager, you obtained 70 per cent of your calories from unrefined carbohydrate, then there is only 30 per cent left to be provided by other things. About 12 per cent would be protein, leaving only 18 per cent for fat and refined carbohydrate. The diet is high in fibre – probably about 100 grams' worth a day – but the fibre is not fighting against huge infusions of fat and sugar. Rather, the unrefined carbohydrate of which the fibre is a part *replaces* fat and carbohydrate. And the hypothesis is that if you eat a diet high in unrefined carbohydrate but low in fat and sugar, then your total intake of calories will be less than if you ate a greater proportion of fat and sugar.

The reason for this has to do with the points outlined above: that calorie intake is not geared exclusively to calorie need, but is influenced by the palatability of food, by the ease with which it is consumed, and by the feeling of satiety it confers.

If diets that are high in unrefined carbohydrate (and low in fat and sugar) are slimming simply because they are unpalatable, then it would be difficult to argue too vigorously in their favour. After all, any food is slimming if you don't like it. You could get remarkably slim on a diet of cream cakes, if you happened to dislike cream cakes.

In truth, advocates of unrefined carbohydrates cannot duck this issue. People eat high-fat and high-sugar foods because they like them: to exclude them is to sacrifice some pleasure. In truth, too, the standard diet of the village African is, by western standards, pretty awful. Even village Africans habitually leave full bowls of food because their jaws begin to ache, and one mealie is very like another. However, diets high in unrefined carbohydrate can be excellent, both varied and flavoursome: and one of the great challenges to the food industry is to use unrefined carbohydrates, in quantity, in ways that are interesting without soaking them in fat and sugar.

The second point, however, is that diets high in unrefined carbohydrates provide fewer total calories because they are harder to consume, and the third is that they tend more easily to induce satiety. It may seem obvious that this is the case: but it is worth, nonetheless, citing evidence in support.

Thus, in one study, reported in 1977 in *The Lancet* by Dr Kenneth Heaton and his colleagues at the University of Bristol, people were asked to eat a certain number of apples as quickly as they could; they averaged 17·2 minutes. But when they were given the same number of calories in the form of apple juice, they swigged it down in only 1·5 minutes. Similarly, in a much older study reported in the 1950s, subjects were able to eat a large amount of wholemeal bread in 45 minutes; but they were able to consume the same number of calories in the form of white bread in only 34 minutes.

Unrefined carbohydrate tends not only to take longer to eat, but also to be more filling. Thus, Dr Heaton and his colleagues found that after subjects had eaten 480 kcal or so in the form of whole apples, they reported feeling much more sated than they did after consuming roughly the same number of calories as apple juice. In another study, subjects who were asked to eat wholemeal bread until they were comfortably full reported that they did indeed feel replete after 665 kcal; but the same subjects, given the same instructions but offered white bread, consumed 825 kcals before they felt full.

Dr Heaton emphasises, however, that it isn't just the presence of fibre that reduces intake, or increases the feeling of satiety. An apple weighing 100 grams (and supplying about 40 kcals) contains only two grams of fibre: a tiny amount which, if simply taken as a spoonful of pure fibre, would have very little influence. But it's the arrangement of the fibre that's important. In its pristine form, wrapped around each apple cell, it converts a quarter of a pound of juice, which you could pour down your throat without noticing, into a solid and indeed challenging object that cannot be consumed without effort. And it is deep in the human psyche, as deep even as greed, to avoid unnecessary work.

Dietary fibre, therefore, in its proper place and with all the caveats outlined above, can help reduce the total amount of energy we consume. But an additional important part of Dr Cleave's original thesis was that it can also reduce the *rate* at which sugars are absorbed from the small intestine. And this, he suggested, was of great significance in yet another disease of affluence, diabetes.

Fibre and diabetes

The concentration of glucose in the blood is normally around 60 to 90 mg per 100 ml. Variation outside this range is certainly acceptable, but if the amount is dramatically high or dramatically low, the result is coma; and, if the concentration is allowed to remain drastically altered, death.

The concentration of blood glucose is regulated by a whole battery of hormones working in concert, but the chief of these is insulin, which is produced by patches of cells (the beta cells, or islets of Langerhans) of the pancreas. Insulin encourages the body tissues to take up glucose. After a meal, therefore, when glucose is infused into the blood from the gut, the beta cells respond by pushing out more insulin, and the rest of the body tissues take up the surplus.

In some people, however, the beta cells may not produce enough insulin, or the insulin may be sabotaged in some way (for example, it may be attacked by antibodies) or the body cells may simply fail to respond to insulin. In such people blood sugar rises uncontrolled. When it reaches 180 mg per 100 ml it spills over into the urine. People who produce a certain amount of sugar in their urine are not necessarily ill; but sugary urine nonetheless signifies diabetes.

Diabetes is a complex disorder but for practical purposes there are two main types: the kind that begins in childhood (juvenile diabetes) and adult-onset diabetes. Adult-onset diabetes is the common form – common, that is, in affluent societies.

There is not, and probably never can be, incontrovertible proof that lack of dietary fibre – or, more generally, a switch from a diet high in unrefined carbohydrate to the modern western diet – is the sole or principal cause of adult-onset diabetes. Three lines of evidence strongly suggest, however, that it might be heavily implicated.

The first is from epidemiology. As Denis Burkitt and Hugh Trowell have often pointed out, adult-onset diabetes is positively rare in rural Africa, but in Britain five per cent of people under the age of 50 excrete sugar in their urine and are in that strict, technical sense 'diabetic' (although this does not necessarily mean that they are ill or need treatment). In over-50s, the proportion rises to 15 per cent. However, between 1941 and 1953 the mortality from diabetes in Britain fell by 54 per cent. Throughout that time, millers were obliged, by law, for reasons of wartime and post-war economy, to provide flour of around 80 per cent extraction, rather than 70 per cent.

The second line of evidence is clinical. More and more doctors are finding that diabetic patients respond well to high-fibre diets: that they need less insulin, and sometimes need no injections at all. We must offer two preliminary points, however. The first is that just because a condition responds well to fibre, it does not mean that lack of fibre caused that disease in the first place. You may treat headache with aspirin, but you would hardly argue that headaches are caused by aspirin-deficiency. However, we are not talking about proof, we are talking about germane observations, in a sphere in which proof will always be elusive.

The second observation is that the high-fibre diets adopted by different doctors are of two quite different types. The first kind of diet has been promoted, in particular, by Dr James W Anderson and his colleagues at the University of Kentucky College of Medicine, Lexington, USA. This diet, at least in overall composition, is very like that of the rural African. It is high in fibre because it provides most of the calories in the form of unrefined carbohydrate – 70 per cent at first (which includes 80 grams of fibre per day), reducing to 55 per cent (providing 52 grams of fibre) for maintenance. The diets worked as was hoped: they reduced the peaks and troughs in blood sugar after meals, and reduced or eliminated the need for injections in most patients. The effect of the diets is not simple to analyse (for example, the patients lost weight, and weight loss may itself benefit some diabetics), but the important point is that it worked.

The second kind of high-fibre diet is far less 'natural', in fact it is not natural at all; and it is unusual in showing how some kinds of fibre can, in some contexts, be used as pharmacological agents. Dr David Jenkins, now at the University of Toronto, reasoned that very viscous forms of fibre should directly reduce the absorption of glucose, just as Cleave hypothesised. And indeed he found that pectins (which, amongst other things, contribute to the viscosity of jam) did indeed suppress the peaks in blood glucose after a meal: but of all such materials, the outstanding form was guar gum. This he gives to diabetic patients incorporated into crispbread. Again, it reduces the need for insulin injections.

Such treatment for diabetes really is revolutionary. Traditionally, diabetics in western societies have been given low-carbohydrate diets in an attempt to reduce their glucose load. This means, incidentally, that diabetics have traditionally eaten high-fat diets: after all, they have to get their energy from somewhere. As I noted on page 64, diabetics are particularly at risk from coronary heart disease. This could, of course, be a direct result of the diabetes, which has many destructive effects, including effects on blood vessels, But it will be interesting to see, as more and more diabetics change from a high-fat diet to one high in unrefined carbohydrate, whether or by how much their risk of heart disease diminishes.

The last line of evidence comes from physiology. Surgeon Captain Cleave suggested many years ago that diabetes might be caused by the body's simple inability to cope with dramatic incursions of glucose from the gut following a sugary meal. He pointed out that in nature, refined carbohydrate is rare; indeed honey is virtually the only source. Only with a modern refined diet are the beta cells ever called upon to cope with sudden, high concentrations of glucose; and eventually, he suggested, they effectively give up. Evidence from Dr Jenkins work, and elsewhere, suggests that this may well be the case.

Thus, with diabetes as with diverticular disease (see below) it seems that people who habitually eat a lot of fibre do not get the disease; that fibre is useful in treating the disease; and that fibre has measurable physiological effects which seem extremely relevant to the disease. In short, the suggestion that a diet high in unrefined carbohydrate and hence high in fibre may help to prevent the disease should not be lightly dismissed.

The effects we have described so far relate to the fore-gut: we have suggested that dietary fibre can reduce total intake of calories and hence militate against obesity, and that it may reduce the rate at which glucose is absorbed and hence militate against diabetes. But the main point of fibre, indeed the definition of fibre, is that it is that portion of the diet not digested by the enzymes produced by the gut, and not absorbed by the small intestine. In other words, dietary fibre – by definition – reaches the colon unchanged. Not surprisingly, it therefore exerts its most obvious effects upon the colon. One reason why dietary fibre is now taken seriously, as was not the case in the past, is that its chemistry is now known to be extremely intricate, and the idea that it might have significant effects is no longer so implausible. Another reason is that the colon itself is now known to be an active, not to say turbulent organ, the activities of which profoundly affect the well-being of the whole body.

Fibre and the colon: constipation, diverticular disease and cancer

The colon is a torrid and active place. Water and minerals, including the vital calcium and potassium, are rescued from it as the food (which finishes up as faeces) passes through. Bile salts, injected into the small intestine from the liver, are broken down when they reach the colon and are to some extent resorbed and then recycled. All these activities are influenced by vast colonies of bacteria – the 'gut flora' – so vast, that their corpses make up most of the dry matter of the faeces.

In this milieu, fibre comes into its own. It reaches the colon unchanged chemically (though knocked about physically) but is then rapidly broken down by the colon bacteria. Even as it is being broken down it acts, in the words of Dr Martin Eastwood of the University of Edinburgh, like a sponge: attracting minerals and water to itself, providing a surface for the bacteria to act on, influencing the kinds of bacteria that may thrive. As it is broken down so its complex carbohydrate structure yields a bewildering range of organic materials, many of which can influence both the bacteria and the activity of the gut wall itself. These materials incidentally include those same volatile fatty acids (VFAs) on which cattle rely. The human colon too can absorb VFAs, and thus fibre, contrary to all received wisdom, provides us with a minor but nonetheless discernible source of energy. The amount of energy absorbed isn't enough to make you fat (though it might be helpful to hunter-gathering people on a marginal diet but with a very high fibre intake) but it does give the lie to the term 'unavailable carbohydrate' by which fibre once was known. Indeed, some of the fibre (lignin) is not carbohydrate, and some of it (which finishes up as VFAs) is not unavailable.

The evidence is growing that this turmoil of activity, in which fibre plays such a central role, has far-reaching consequences. An obvious and immediate consequence is that fibre increases the mass and the bulk of the stools. Village Africans, on their diet of roots (cassava), maize and beans, produce about 400 grams of faeces per day. Furthermore, those faeces are soft and float on water (not least because they contain bubbles of gas). By contrast, the average westerner produces only 100 grams of faeces per day, which characteristically are hard and sink in water. Dr

Denis Burkitt is fond of remarking that if only people could be induced to produce floating stools, then half the world's health problems would be solved; though a sanitary engineer to whom the point was put pointed out that this would complicate his life no end.

The increase in faecal bulk and mass clearly does not simply reflect the added weight of fibre. Thus, Dr John Cummings at Cambridge found that whereas people produced less than 80 grams of faeces per day when they ate only 17 grams of cereal bran, they managed nearly 230 grams a day when eating 40 grams of bran. The increase in weight comes primarily from an extra mass of bacteria, which thrive upon the fibre. However, different kinds of fibre clearly have very different effects on stool weight (though the precise difference that each kind makes varies from individual to individual – presumably because of individual differences in gut flora). Bran is particularly effective in increasing stool weight. Other kinds of fibre are much less so. One American trial, however, did show that people could increase stool weight from less than 90 to more than 200 grams per day by eating a wide variety of fruits and vegetables in what was described as 'a very acceptable diet'.

Increasing the mass of faeces may not, in itself, seem terribly helpful. It may even seem unsavoury (and Dr Eastwood has pleasant anecdotes of trials that had to be called off as particular apportionments of fibre proved too effective). On the matter of aesthetics, however, Dr Burkitt suggests that the soft inverted mushroom produced by the rural African is a more pleasing object than the inspissated western creation, and Jonathan Swift, whose aversion to living things in general was partly prompted by their production of faeces in particular, was known to make an exception of the horse, whose excrements he found perfectly acceptable.

Aesthetics are a diversion, however. Closer to our theme is that in people who produce a high mass of soft stools, the food also passes through the gut much more quickly: that is, the 'transit time' is reduced. Thus, in rural Africans, food passes right through the gut in around 35 hours (or, in some cases, far less). In westerners, transit times are nearer 100 hours.

The clinical relevance even of these three observations – increased stool mass; production of softer stools; and decreased transit time – could alone be highly significant. It seems almost self-evident, for example (it isn't quite self-evident; but the caveats are not really worth bothering with), that fibre will relieve constipation, and, more to the point, prevent it occurring in the first place. There has been a fashion among doctors for suggesting that constipation *per se* does not really matter. Nonetheless there are plenty of reasons for thinking it undesirable, and the fact is that laxatives are among the western world's minor boom industries.

And constipation clearly can be serious. Apart from anything else, it is apparently the underlying cause of diverticular disease of the colon (see Figure 7). In this condition the muscular wall of the gut ruptures, generally in many places, and the lining of the colon (which should of course be on the inside) balloons outwards through the ruptures, to produce a series of pockets, or diverticulae. The pockets are generally small – some too small for the naked eye – but the largest ones may be a centimetre across.

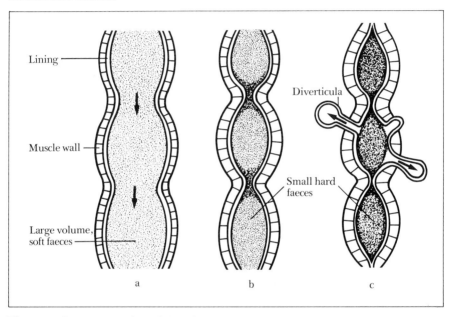

Figure 7 *Cross-sections through the colon:*

(a) *On a high-fibre diet the high-volume, soft faecal content is propelled along easily.*

(b) *On a low-fibre diet the small, hard faecal content needs extra effort from the muscles in the bowel wall which becomes stronger.*

(c) *These increased pressures can eventually force pouches of the lining through the muscle wall. These are the diverticula.*

These diverticulae are common: in western countries, they are present in about 10 per cent of men and women over 40. In most people they remain merely as curiosities, but in some they become inflamed. At the least, the inflammation is painful: more seriously the inflamed diverticulae may lead to abscesses and obstruct the gut; indeed, it's because such events intervene that the diverticulae do not grow beyond a centimetre or so. Other organs, including the bladder, may become involved. In some cases surgery is the only recourse and in some the disease eventually leads to a painful death.

But in countries with a high intake of fibre, diverticular disease is rare. In fact, among traditional communities in Africa south of the Sahara it is virtually unknown. The reason, again, is nothing to do with race: a recent study from Baragwanath Hospital, Johannesburg, shows an increasing incidence among blacks who had been eating a westernised diet for around 20 years. Again, mere association between a certain diet and a particular condition does not indicate cause, but in this case (as in the case of fat and atheroma) there is good reason to suppose that lack of fibre genuinely is the reason why diverticular disease develops.

The physiological explanation is, it seems, largely a matter of simple mechanics. It is the task of the colon to push faeces along its length, which it does by sending waves of muscular contraction from the front to the rear – an action known as peristalsis. Muscles, as everyone knows, are remarkably accommodating. Those in the top of the arm, for example, double or halve their length as you reach to find a new piece of paper for the typewriter, and clearly they can contract either when bunched up or extended.

But muscles, nevertheless, have an optimum length, which they prefer. They do not like to be too stretched, or too bunched up: at extremes, they lose efficiency. The muscles of the wall of the colon are designed by nature to be fairly relaxed to form a good-sized circumference, which they can be, if the faeces are bulky. But if the faeces are small and hard then the colon must squeeze in further than its muscular walls can comfortably manage. The tension is too great, and the pressure within the lumen is too high (as has indeed been measured). This overcontraction, over many years, leads to ruptures.

Such an explanation may seem obvious, even simplistic. The irony is, however, that for many years doctors recommended that patients with diverticular disease should adopt a *low*-fibre diet. They argued that because fibrous food tends to be hard, and because it was known that fibre reaches the gut chemically unchanged, then fibre in the diet would further irritate a bowel that was already inflamed. Now (thanks not least to the pioneer observations outlined by Cleave, Campbell and Painter) doctors recommend a high-fibre diet to treat this disease; and many hospitals where this is done have found that surgery for the condition is often, indeed usually, unnecessary. Of course, as noted above, the fact that treating the condition with fibre is effective does not prove that lack of fibre caused the condition in the first place. But the fact that the treatment works fits in neatly with the observation that people who habitually eat a high-fibre diet do not get the disease, and with the physiological explanation of the events that cause the disease. The real irony, perhaps, is that hard, fibrous food does not produce hard, fibrous faeces – in fact its result is precisely opposite. To use the phrase Kenneth Heaton has coined, 'hard in, soft out!'

The most serious of all diseases of the colon is, of course, cancer of the colon. This again is a western disease. In New England (Connecticut) and in Scotland, the rate among men aged 30 to 65 is more than 51 per 100,000. The figure reported for New York incidentally is lower (around 45) and England is also lower than Scotland – but the figures nonetheless are high. Contrast them with South Saharan African statistics: 3·5 per 100,000 in Uganda; 5·5 per 100,000 in Mozambique; 5·9 per 100,000 in Nigeria. The places you might expect to be in between are in between: Bombay (which is high by Indian standards) 14·6 per 100,000; Yugoslavia and Bulgaria around 20 per 100,000.

Again, diet emerges as the crucial factor. Again we might point out that fibre is not the only difference between the diets of people with different rates of this particular disease – and indeed, cancer of the colon is associated with a high-fat diet, just as much as with a low-fibre diet.

In short, it is not established beyond all reasonable doubt that lack of dietary fibre is the cause (certainly not that it is the sole cause) of cancer of the colon. But the idea that it might be one cause, and an important one at that, is entirely plausible; and again we must ask whether it is appropriate to be purist and to demand 'proof', or whether it is appropriate to take action against a serious, indeed deadly, disease on the basis of that plausibility. Doctors must make such decisions on behalf of their patients; individuals must make them for themselves. But two arguments at least, proposed by Denis Burkitt among others, suggest that lack of fibre might indeed by seriously implicated.

The first is that colonic cancer presumably (and experimental evidence suggests undoubtedly) arises from contact with the bowel contents. We know that the chemical composition of the bowel contents is largely determined by the bacteria in the bowel. It's known, too, that among the many hundreds of organic compounds those bacteria can produce are some that, in laboratory experiments, can be shown to have at least some of the properties known to promote cancer. It's also established that when the diet is low in fibre, the faeces remain in the bowel longer – which means that the gut flora have a greater time to work on those contents, and a greater opportunity to generate cancer-promoting materials. This scenario is unproven; but each of the steps can be demonstrated, and the overall pattern is entirely logical.

The association between cancer of the colon and a high-fat diet is not, of course, incompatible with the idea that fibre deficiency is also important. It may well be that fat helps to cause the cancer (perhaps by providing raw materials for the bacteria to work upon) while fibre is preventive, in which case too much fat and too little fibre would work hand in hand.

In general, of course, it is not too difficult to see how fibre could affect the colon: the colon, after all, is fibre's chief theatre of action. But the advocates of high-fibre diets also suggest that it may help to prevent diseases such as gallstones, diabetes and coronary heart disease where the connection seems more remote. How come?

Fibre and gallstones

One of the most bizarre inventions in the human body is bile. It is produced in the liver, stored in a little bag known as the gall bladder, and squirted into the duodenum, via the bile duct, after meals. It contains pigments, which are of no great importance to our story, and salts, which are. These salts are derived from cholesterol and act as detergent. Once inside the small intestine they help to emulsify the fat in the food: that is, to break it into very small globules, which can be held in suspension in the watery surroundings, like oil is held in French dressing. In addition, the cholesterol-derived bile salts help to hold cholesterol itself in suspension: and surplus cholesterol is excreted, from the liver, via the bile.

After the bile salts have fulfilled their detergent function in the small intestine, they pass on down to the large intestine. There they are acted upon and chemically modified by the bowel bacteria. Some of the bile salts, to some degree modified, are then resorbed and live to fight another day: they find their way back to the liver and again are incorporated into bile. The rest of the salts pass on through the colon and are excreted in the faeces.

Sometimes, and for some reason particularly in women, stones form in the gall bladder. The stones may have various origins, but the commonest is cholesterol itself: it crystallises out. It can do this for two reasons. First, the liver may simply put more cholesterol into the bile than the bile can accommodate. Or, secondly, the bile salts may be deficient, or chemically altered so that they no longer fulfil their detergent function so efficiently.

Usually these gallstones cause no trouble. But sometimes they lodge in the bile duct where, depending on their exact position, they may either cause great pain or may prevent the secretion of bile altogether. In the latter case, the bile spreads around the whole body to produce jaundice. Gallstones, then, can be extremely painful, frequently require surgery and can even be fatal.

Gallstones qualify as a disease of affluence. They are common in western countries and, as Denis Burkitt points out, they are rarely seen in hospitals serving rural Africa. Again, as with cancer of the colon, there is a very intriguing relationship between incidence of gallstones and the amount of fibre in the diet: the less the fibre, the more the gallstones. In this case, however, it may seem harder to find a plausible relationship. How on earth can fibre in the diet influence the excretion of cholesterol, or the behaviour of bile salts?

The answer is that there are several ways, and for some at least of these there is incontrovertible experimental evidence. For one thing (though this is probably not outstandingly important) the presence of fibre in the small intestine may inhibit the absorption of cholesterol and fat, and so reduce the load of cholesterol that the liver has to deal with.

But the influence of fibre on the bile salts themselves may be more important. Fibre in the colon may bind the bile salts and simply prevent their resorption; they pass out with the faeces instead. This means, of course, that they cannot be resorbed and so recycled. Hence the liver has to manufacture more bile salts. And bile salts, as we have mentioned, are synthesised from cholesterol; and so more cholesterol is used up.

Dr Kenneth Heaton has shown yet another mechanism. The bile salts, as we said, are chemically altered in the colon by bacteria before they are resorbed. But the presence of fibre greatly modifies the action of those bacteria. When fibre is present, the modification of bile salts is such that it does not impair their function: when they are resorbed, they work just as well when reincorporated into bile as they did first time round. But in the absence of fibre, the colonic bacteria have a more destructive action. The bile salts are chemically altered in such a way that, when they are resorbed and reincorporated into the bile, they no longer function so efficiently as detergent. Thus the bile cannot accommodate cholesterol as readily as it should; so the surplus cholesterol forms crystals.

The story is confusing: it seems perverse of the body to make salts out of cholesterol in order to dissolve more cholesterol. The effect of bacteria in the presence or absence of fibre may seem unlikely. The facts, however, in this apparently contrived story, are established.

Thus, again, we do not have proof beyond reasonable doubt that absence of fibre is the sole or principal cause of gallstones. We do have intriguing evidence that the two may be connected, and sound physiological reasons for thinking that fibre might indeed affect cholesterol metabolism.

Fibre and coronary heart disease

Clearly, material that promotes the turnover of cholesterol and promotes its excretion ought to be helpful in reducing the risk of coronary heart disease. This is not to suggest that there is direct evidence that it does; merely that the idea is by no means foolish. Again I may quote the studies by James W Anderson and his colleagues of the University of Kentucky. To recap: they put some of their diabetic patients on diets providing no less than 70 per cent of daily calories as unrefined carbohydrate, which involves a daily fibre intake of more than 80 grams. Within five days the patient's serum cholesterol levels had fallen by 20 per cent, and they fell by a further five per cent over the next five days. In the longer term the patients went on to a maintenance diet, in which 55 per cent of calories were supplied as unrefined carbohydrate, with 52 grams of fibre per day. After 19 months their low cholesterol levels were maintained; indeed they fell from a mean of 222 mg per 100 ml (which, as described on page 56, is roughly average for middle-aged western men) down to 188 mg per 100 ml. Furthermore, the HDL/LDL ratio (see page 47) had improved markedly. Indeed, HDL levels (included in the total figure of 188 mg per cent) had doubled.

Dr Anderson points out that this reduction in cholesterol cannot be ascribed solely to increase in fibre intake. These diabetic patients were also on a very low fat intake – only 11 per cent at first, rising to 26 per cent in the maintenance diet. However, we may again note that a diet in which most of the energy comes from unrefined carbohydrate is bound to be low in fat. More specifically, however, studies at Kentucky have shown that oat bran given to rats does seem both to reduce LDLs and raise HDLs. These are early days to make general pronouncements, but the preliminary observation is that dietary fibre does seem to have a specifically favourable effect on serum cholesterol, quite apart from the simple replacement of fat with carbohydrate.

Taken all in all, then, the increasing emphasis on unrefined carbohydrate may be seen as the mirror image of the increasing disaffection with fat: as the latter goes down, so the former should increase. In addition, specific forms of fibre seem to have specific, salutory effects, and the time may come when nutritionists can offer detailed and wide-ranging instruction on which particular fibres to eat for which particular purpose; just as they may, one day, offer detailed instruction with respect to polyunsaturated fats. In the meantime, one task is to provide high-fibre (and low-fat, low-sugar) meals which are pleasant to eat, and which people are prepared to eat habitually. The African village diet may not be too alluring, but a little ingenuity applied to the world's cuisines might solve some of man's outstanding problems.

HOW MUCH FIBRE ARE YOU EATING?

Increase fibre intake
to 30g per day

The following table gives the major sources of fibre in the British diet. They have been divided into units that will each provide approximately 3g of fibre. Therefore, to meet the NACNE recommendations you should try to eat at least *10 portions* a day. (Any foods not on the list are not particularly rich in fibre.)

Fill in the boxes with the number of servings you eat in a day and add them up. If your total falls short of 10, use the list to choose new foods to add to your daily diet.

Breakfast Cereals	How many servings (1 small cereal bowl)?
Allbran (counts as 2 servings)	☐
Bran Buds (counts as 2 servings)	☐
Honey and Nut Farmhouse Bran (counts as 2 servings)	☐
Muesli	☐
Shredded Wheat	☐
Shreddies	☐
Toasted Farmhouse Bran with Apple and Banana (counts as 2 servings)	☐
Weetabix	☐
Weeta Flakes	☐

Bread and Starch foods	How many slices or portions?
Bread	☐
Hi Bran	☐
Hovis (2 slices equivalent to 1 serving)	☐
Wheatmeal (2 slices equivalent to 1 serving)	☐
Wholemeal	☐
Wholemeal Spaghetti	☐
Other wholemeal pasta	☐

Fresh Fruit	How many fruits or servings?
Apples	☐
Bananas	☐
Blackberries	☐
Bread fruit	☐
Guavas	☐
Loganberries	☐
Oranges	☐
Passion fruit	☐
Raspberries	☐
Red/blackcurrants	☐
Rhubarb	☐

Dried Fruit	How many tablespoons?
Apricots	☐
Currants	☐
Dates	☐
Figs	☐
Prunes	☐
Raisins	☐
Sultanas	☐

Vegetables	How many large heaped tablespoons or equivalent?
Aubergine	☐
Baked beans	☐
Beansprouts	☐
Beetroot	☐
Broad beans	☐
Broccoli	☐
Brown rice	☐
Brussels sprouts	☐
Butter beans	☐
Cabbage	☐
Carrots	☐
Celeriac	☐
Chick peas	☐
Kidney beans	☐

Vegetables continued	How many heaped tablespoons or equivalent
Leeks	☐
Lentils (cooked)	☐
Mushrooms	☐
Okra	☐
Parsnips	☐
Peas	☐
Pigeon peas	☐
Plantain	☐
Potatoes (boiled in skins)	☐
Potatoes (jacket)	☐
Red beans	☐
Runner beans	☐
Spinach	☐
Spring greens	☐
Spring onions	☐
Swedes	☐
Sweetcorn	☐
Turnips	☐
Yams	☐

Nuts	How many large heaped tablespoons or equivalent?
Almonds	☐
Brazils	☐
Chestnuts	☐
Coconut	☐
Hazelnuts	☐
Peanuts (fresh or roasted)	☐
Walnuts	☐

Total _____

Chapter 7

THE MYTHOLOGY OF PROTEIN

If our culture were geared towards science: if the headlines of the daily newspapers dealt as a matter of course with the affairs of science and not, apparently as a matter of duty, exclusively with the to-ings and fro-ings of politicians, then it would be acknowledged that one of the most significant economic developments in the twentieth century has been the rise and fall of the importance attached to protein. From World War II until well into the 1960s, nutritionists, agriculturalists and politicians alike accepted that human beings needed to eat huge amounts of protein; not only huge amounts, but protein of the finest quality – obtainable, so it seemed, only from animal products. This could best be done (it seemed) by concentrating agricultural resource on producing livestock. It was seen to be right and proper (and not just commercially advantageous) to grow wheat, barley, maize and beans not for eating but to feed to cattle, pigs and poultry. It was held to be self-evident that many Third World countries, if not most, could not possibly produce enough protein to maintain their swelling populations, and that those countries must therefore forever be beholden to the cornfields of the west, which in practice meant North America.

Then, throughout the 1970s, opinion changed. It was perceived that people did not need as much protein as had been thought. Furthermore, there was no reason to fret too much about quality; a suitable mixture of plant proteins was generally good enough. Indeed it suddenly became clear that all the world's major staple foods, the cereals, the pulses, and even the roots and tubers such as potatoes, could comfortably provide all or most of people's daily protein; and the principal nutritional role for animal products should be only to provide various vitamins and minerals, and some essential fats. It became clear that instead of growing cereal just to feed cattle and pigs, it would be better simply to eat it. With this single modification in nutritional theory the prospects for all humankind were changed. Suddenly it was obvious that the present world population could be fed, and fed several times over. It was clear, too, that most Third World countries could, in theory, easily grow enough food for themselves; there was no thereotical need for them to rely upon any other country. No event since the Second World War, I humbly submit, not the Berlin wall, nor the birth of the EEC, nor even the revolutions in China, has quite the resonance for all humankind as the simple realisation that we were going the wrong way about feeding ourselves; and the corresponding realisation that if we went about things the right way, then feeding people was – technically – easy (as I discussed in *The Famine Business*, Pelican, 1979).

How did protein acquire such importance?

It isn't hard to see why nutritionists began, as this century wore on, to attach more and more importance to protein. It is the principal component of flesh; and not just of flesh (muscle) but of all body organs, skin, hair and nails. All enzymes are proteins, and enzymes are the catalysts that regulate all of life's activities. The turnover of protein is very rapid: all of the body cells are constantly being taken apart and put together again ('wear and tear') and the enzymes themselves are used only a few times (or probably, in reality, a few hundred or thousand times), and then broken down and reconstructed from fresh materials. For young animals, of course, protein for growth must be added to normal turnover. Yet the body does not store protein, as it stores fat, to be called upon when supplies run low: all the protein in the body at any one time is serving some specific purpose, as a structural component of some tissue or as an enzyme or – as is common – as both. On purely theoretical grounds, then, it is obvious that the body needs a constant supply of protein. That, of course, will never be in dispute: the only questions concern the amount and the quality required.

The reasons protein requirements became so exaggerated in the decades after the Second World War were a combination of excellent field research, a desire to do good, bad luck and commercial opportunism. The excellent pioneer field research was carried out in West Africa in the 1930s by Dr Cicely Williams. She observed the condition in toddlers known as *kwashiorkor*: the skin becomes dry and scaly, the hair becomes reddish, and the belly is swollen. Children with kwashiorkor can look bonny: their eyes are large and their contours are rounded. But the condition is highly dangerous, and the prognosis for a child with kwashiorkor is often far worse than for children who are more obviously starved and look emaciated. The round belly and the smooth contours are filled out not by fat, but by dropsy; the condition reflects metabolism in extreme disarray. Dr Williams suggested a cause: 'some amino acid or protein deficiency cannot be excluded'. This insight remains, in outline, valid. It was a fine piece of work.

The bad luck that intervened was the outbreak of the Second World War. Then, virtually all such field research came to a stop. When the war ended, the United Nations was born with a mandate to do good. High among the priorities was the desire to feed the world's hungry. But what, specifically, did hungry people lack? Conspicuous among nutritional disorders was kwashiorkor: indeed by 1953 the Food and Agriculture Organisation of the United Nations (FAO) had concluded that kwashiorkor was 'the most serious and widespread nutritional disorder known to medical and nutritional science'. What caused it? There was the research from the 1930s, suggesting a lack of protein, and little time for much reflection. Lack of protein was accepted as the cause – and lack of protein therefore must be a serious, indeed the principal, nutritional problem worldwide.

Enter, commercial opportunism. You can make a reasonable living by growing cereal and selling it to people to make bread. But you can make far, far more by feeding the bulk of that cereal to livestock, and then selling meat, or eggs, or butter and cheese. Indeed, there's a limit to the amount of cereal people can eat, but there is no theoretical limit to their ability to get through livestock. In addition, the agriculture both of the US and of Britain was ebullient in the decades after the war. The US at last had the machines to conquer its enormous territories and had the political and commercial clout needed to export: and the UK was resolved never again to allow its agriculture to run down, as it had in the 1930s, and leave itself open to blockade. The general idea that protein was the key component of diet, that people needed a lot of it, and that the prime task of agriculture should therefore be to produce as much of the highest quality protein as possible, gave a deep, moral respectability to barley beef, battery chickens and the Friesian dairy cattle, which, in some American states, stretched to the horizon.

What is the truth?

It's hard to see exactly where the disillusionment about protein crept in. It actually had several sources, the first being the realisation that the protein story itself is not quite as simple as it once seemed.

There are, basically, three things worth saying about protein. The first is that people do indeed need a basic minimum amount – an absolute quantity, measurable in grams per day. The second is that it is important to maintain a proper balance of protein to total energy. And the third is that protein does indeed vary in nutritional value (that is, in 'quality') and it is necessary not only to have enough, but to have enough of the right grade. I'll look at each of these three points briefly in turn.

I will not dwell in detail on the absolute amounts of protein in grams per kilogram of body weight per day that various international and national bodies have recommended these past few decades. Suffice to say that in 1948, when protein was in the ascendant, the National Research Council of the United States recommended a protein intake for small children that was almost precisely twice what was recommended by Britain's Department of Health and Social Security in 1969; and that the amount recommended by the FAO and the World Health Organisation, albeit for adults rather than children, is now about half that DHSS figure. The practical significance of this is that it would have been hard to meet the NRC's 1948 recommendation without heavy reliance on animal products, or particularly rich plant sources such as soya. To meet present requirements, you need use animal products only to supplement plant protein – or indeed, as vegans demonstrate, you do not require them as a protein source at all.

The question of the protein: energy ratio is subtle. One possibly minor but intriguing point is that when you take in food (energy) the body has to deal with it. It has to digest it, absorb it, turn it into glycogen or fat, or burn it off in the form of heat. All this (with the exception of absorption) is done by enzymes, which are proteins and which need constant renewal. A diet consisting only of energy-rich foods, such as sugar or fat, would leave you eventually without the means to process that food.

That first point applies to all diets, however much energy you are taking in. A second point to do with ratio applies primarily to diets where the intake of energy is marginal, or low. If a person, for example, an African child, is not taking in enough energy, then he or she will begin to use the body's own protein as 'fuel'. The protein in muscle tissue can, after all, be converted by devious routes into carbohydrate and then 'burnt'. Because of this, a diet low in energy can lead to protein deficiency. On the specific matter of kawashiorkor, it's clear that a high-protein diet is useful in treatment; but few would argue that a lack of protein specifically leads to the condition in the first place. Far more common is a lack of protein *and energy*: it's because the energy is lacking that the body protein is sacrificed.

Now we come to a point also picked up in Chapter 6 on carbohydrates. This is that, whereas carbohydrate in the form of sugar is not accompanied by protein (it is 'pure energy'), the carbohydrate (starch) that is contained in cereals, or pulses, or potatoes or cassava, *is*. Cereals and pulses are, after all, seeds and are meant to nourish the embryo plant: and the potato, a tuber, is a substitute seed, with the task of nourishing the next generation of potatoes. The seed must provide the embryo plant with a complete 'diet' until it can feed itself. Animal bodies do not store surplus protein, but plant seeds do – they turn out a wide range of 'storage proteins'. Indeed the ratio of protein to energy in cereals, pulses, or even in potatoes is not very different from what modern nutritionists recommend for humans. If your diet consisted mainly of cereal, then you need be deficient neither in protein nor energy; putting it another way, if you ate enough cereal to provide your daily energy needs, then you would automatically acquire enough protein.

Two consequences of this line of thought are worth pursuing. The first is that, in general, the hungry people of the world, including the children with kwashiorkor, are not specifically short of protein: they are short of *food*. Whatever it is they eat naturally they should (in general) be given more of and should not (in general) be laden with high-protein imported supplements as has commonly been the policy. There is one very large caveat, however. This is that a diet very high in cereals, particularly the less highly bred cereals such as sorghum, or high in staples such as the root cassava, are extremely bulky: they have a high content of fibre and (in the case of cassava) water. This may be fine for adults with well developed teeth, who have stopped growing: the high-fibre, high-bulk diet helps to keep them slim, as discussed on page 94. But it may not be so good for children, or for lactating mothers, who may not be able to eat enough such bulky food in a day to grow or to feed an infant respectively. One point of all this is that in saying that livestock, in recent decades, has been over-emphasised, I do not mean to suggest (as some have somewhat precipitately suggested) that livestock has no role. For us westerners, worried about waistlines and coronary heart disease, the high concentration of energy (fat) and protein in animal food may be pernicious. But people on marginal diets, particularly children and lactating mothers, may well benefit greatly from animal supplements, without which they may be hard-pressed to take in enough food.

The second consequence worth a thought is that in western societies, rather than in poor countries, it is at least theoretically possible to have a diet with a low ratio of protein to energy simply by eating huge amounts of energy without corresponding protein. I wonder vaguely (though without knowledge of any evidence on the point) whether the extremely fat children who once were conspicuous in the United States came into this category: their protein was confined to hamburgers and the small amount in their potato crisps (known in the US as chips); but their energy was ingested in the form of massive infusions of fat and sugar from endless milk shakes and fizzy drinks. Taken all in all, then, there are various ways of getting protein, or protein: energy, wrong.

It is theoretically possible to take in adequate energy and yet have an *absolute* deficiency of protein: that is, take in fewer grams per day than the FAO says is adequate. This possible state was previously thought to be common in the Third World and to be the root cause of kwashiorkor. It now seems, however, that to have an adequate energy intake and yet have an absolute deficiency of protein must be a rare condition. Far more common is to be deficient both in protein *and* in energy; or to have an intake of protein that is theoretically adequate and yet take in too little energy, so that the protein is burnt to provide energy. Either or both of these patterns probably lie at the root of kwashiorkor.

In affluent societies, two kinds of excess are possible. One is simply to take in far more protein than your body needs and also (the two would probably go together) to take in a higher ratio of protein to energy than your body needs. A gross surplus of protein may not be harmful (except in the case of some specific pathological conditions), though there is some evidence that protein surplus may encourage obesity, not by providing excess calories but by encouraging the laying down of fat. In world terms, however, intake of surplus protein is quite simply greedy – the surplus is just 'burned' off as energy; and, as we will discuss below, protein is in practice associated with undesirable nutrients, such as saturated fat.

Finally, as in the case of the hypothetical child living on hamburgers, crisps and fizzy drinks, it is theoretically possible to have an adequate basic minimum intake of protein and yet have a low ratio of protein to energy. However, though I personally find such musing interesting, it is not vital to our theme. The final topic we should look at briefly here is that of protein quality.

Proteins are constructed from amino acids: indeed they are chains of amino acids. In nature there are about 20 amino acids, though others can be synthesised in the laboratory. Most of the natural amino acids the body can make for itself – from other amino acids. The common amino acid glycine, for example, can be made in the body from any other amino acid you care to eat. However, eight of the 20 amino acids have to be supplied ready made in the food: these are the so-called essential amino acids. The essential amino acids are made only in plants; carnivorous animals obtain them by eating other animals which in turn have eaten plants.

In order to make all the proteins it needs, then, the body must be supplied with all the essential amino acids, in a correct ratio one to another. If any one essential amino acid is lacking, then protein production cannot go ahead. Generous supplies of other essential amino acids will not meet the case. After all, a lack of steering wheels could bring a motor-car factory to a halt; and a train-load of gear levers, though equally desirable in their way, would not make up the difference.

Most of the proteins in food do not contain an ideal ratio of essential amino acids. Very few food proteins are totally deficient in any one essential amino acid, but many are *relatively* deficient in at least one; and if any one is to some extent lacking, then the rest are to that extent wasted, just as the train-load of gear-levers would be wasted if there was a lack of steering wheels.

In the past, nutritionists made much of this variation in quality. Indeed they glibly, and it now seems erroneously, divided proteins into 'first class' – those that were well primed in all essential amino acids – and 'second class' – those with conspicuous deficiencies in one or more essential amino acids. Worse, there was a tendency to equate 'first class' with 'animal', and 'second class' with 'plant'. Thus at one time books on nutrition virtually ignored the protein content of wheat and were content to give the impression that flour should be equated solely with starch.

Now the heat has gone out of this discussion. It's clear, for one thing, that the quality of many plant proteins (including that of soya and various other beans) is very high; higher than that of many animal proteins. The bland relegation of plant proteins is obviously inappropriate. It's clear, too, that as human beings do not apparently need as much protein as once was though, then quality is not, usually, a burning issue.

Thus is you were eating a protein that contained only 80 per cent as much lysine as is required but a satisfactory quantity of all the other essential amino acids rating of 80 per cent: the lack of lysine would drag the rest down. But if you ate 25 per cent more of that protein than you actually 'required', then you would be taking in as much lysine as you needed, with the rest of the amino acids in slight, but unharmful, surplus; and all the body cares about is that it has enough protein of appropriate quality.

Lysine, in fact, is the essential amino acid that is most likely to be lacking in cereal proteins; and this has caused nutritionists much angst, and prompted plant breeders to seek to develop high-lysine varieties, notably of barley. However, one of nature's many serendipities is that it has supplied pulses (beans) with a surplus of lysine. Thus if you eat cereals *and* beans, the lack of essential amino acid in the one is made up by the surfeit in the other. In general, nutritionists nowadays prudently recommend eating a mixture of plant proteins; and in particular, we find that the cereal-with-pulse theme runs right through the world's great cuisines, from chapati with dhall in India, to houmous (made from chick peas) with pitta bread around the Mediterranean, to beans on toast in Britain.

Taken all in all, then, the emphasis of nutritional theory is no longer upon protein. No longer are we encouraged to eat a great deal of it; no longer is it suggested that meat, eggs and dairy products should provide the bulk of what we need. Indeed the current view is diametrically different. As described in Chapter 5, an excess of saturated fat is now firmly discouraged: and as Britain's NACNE report points out, many of the foods that in the past were recommended as high-protein foods are now to be played down, because they are also high-fat foods.

The point is epitomised by cheddar cheese, for years extolled as the embodiment of milk, and hence of all that was nourishing, especially protein. Indeed it is high in protein – it is 26% protein by weight, which puts it on a par with lean rump steak. But no less than 33% of its weight is fat. Cheddar also has an appreciable content of water (about 37%). This means that almost half of the solid material in cheddar cheese is fat, and as fat is highly calorific, it accordingly supplies a large proportion of the total energy in cheese – two thirds, in fact. As we are now being urged to derive only about 30% of our calories from fat, it's clear that cheddar is among the foods to be taken in modest amounts (although, with its impressive content of calcium and its powerful flavour, it still deserves a place in our diet).

In addition, as described in Chapter 6, the emphasis now is on obtaining a large proportion of our energy – as large a proportion as one might reasonably tolerate, indeed – from unrefined carbohydrate foods and, in particular, from cereals, abetted by pulses. If we do not eat enough cereals to supply the bulk of our energy then, as we have seen, we would automatically obtain enough protein.

In short, the recommenation throughout this book is to shift the balance of diet towards what is still common in Mediterranean and Eastern countries: a high proportion of cereals, pulses, vegetables and fruit; and small amounts of meat and fish used for flavour and garnish. If we pursue such a diet, then protein will take care of itself. Officiously to seek out high-protein foods is to tread the dangerous path to high fat and low fibre.

Chapter 8

VITAMINS
AND MINERALS

In each chapter of this book, whether we've been considering fat or fibre
or protein or what it really means to be an omnivore, the same kind of
recommendations have been arrived at: that human beings should
derive the bulk of their energy from unrefined carbohydrates, which in
general means plants and in practice primarily means cereals (with
pulses, vegetables and fruit in lavish attendance); that meat, fish and
other animal products should be eaten sparingly, as garnish, as in the
cuisines of the Mediterranean and the East; and that within these
generous confines, modern civilised human beings, like their
hunter-gatherer ancestors, should seek variety. These principles apply in
this chapter, too: if pursued successfully, then vitamins would take care
of themselves.

That ought to be the end of the chapter, but a few points do seem to
be in order. For one thing, it is perfectly clear that not everyone in our
society does pursue the ideals. In truth, obvious vitamin-deficiency
disease in Britain seems to occur only in special circumstances. Thus
alcoholic vagrants may be severely deficient in niacin and other B
vitamins, with the associated chapped lips and sore tongue that
represent the early stages of pellagra; and sometimes, too, they show
distinct signs of scurvy, associated with a lack of ascorbic acid (vitamin
C). But among people whose lives are not so obviously disastrous,
obvious vitamin disease has recently been reported only among some
immigrants, whose children have sometimes developed rickets caused by
a lack of vitamin D. The reason, so various analyses suggest, is
compound. It is probably in part dietary – in general from an attempt to
pursue a traditional diet in an alien country – and in part cultural. The
point here is that vitamin D is one of the few vitamins the human body
can synthesise itself, but to do this it needs exposure to sunlight. Some
Asian groups, in particular, tend to eschew the sun, swaddling their
babies, covering their own bodies from head to toe, and spending a lot of
time indoors. In countries where the sun is excessive no harm results;

but in countries where the apportionment of sunshine is niggardly it pays to take advantage of what there is.

Some vitamins, too, which ought to take care of themselves, are extremely fragile. Thus vitamin C is found in fresh vegetables and some fruits, such as oranges and, above all, blackcurrants, are awash with it. But the most important single source of vitamin C for people in Britain is the potato. It's not that potatoes are particularly rich in the vitamin, but people do eat a great many of them, whereas they don't eat huge amounts of blackcurrants.

But vitamin C doesn't like being kept waiting around; it doesn't like being heated, particularly for long periods; and it is readily oxidised when exposed to air. So old potatoes contain less vitamin C than new ones, and the longer they are stored, the less they contain. By late spring, before the new crop comes in, their content is positively feeble. The traditional fate of the old potato is either to be made into chips (French fries), or to be boiled. Deep frying is not as destructive of vitamin C as boiling, because it's quicker. But the chip or the boiled potato as served in the average canteen is left to sit for minutes or even hours, warming through, as the customers file past with their trays; and with each passing minute the ascorbate breaks down. Mashing the potatoes introduces air and encourages oxidation, so reducing the C content even more. The amount of vitamin C needed to avoid scurvy is very low and easily obtained; one really would not expect to see scurvy in a civilised society under normal circumstances. But many nutritionists would argue that the amount needed to avoid scurvy is less than a person *should* ideally ingest; and observation suggests that an intake of vitamin C hardly better than marginal must be commonplace.

Occasionally, evidence accrues to suggest that marginal deficiencies, caused by precisely the kinds of circumstance outlined above, may have serious consequences. Britain's Medical Research Council is now conducting trials to test the hypothesis that spina bifida may be caused by a deficiency of yet another B vitamin, folic acid, during the first few days of embryonic development. Some would suggest that the case is already made: trials in Leeds and elsewhere suggest that supplements of folic acid (and other vitamins) before pregnancy reduce the incidence of this birth defect. The prevailing feeling is that the case must be proved beyond all reasonable doubt before a campaign to promote the vitamin is undertaken. But no-one (least of all those who are conducting the trial) would doubt that the case implicating folic acid deficiency must be taken very seriously indeed.

But why should women eating an unexceptional British diet be deficient in folic acid? The vitamin is contained in two main categories of food: liver, which is the richest source, and green vegetables. Endive, for some reason, is remarkably endowed, and fresh peas and chick peas are also very good sources. In practice, however, most people do not eat liver regularly, so green vegetables are the principal source. But green vegetables, unfortunately, are one of the first items to be put to one side in times of economic stringency. In addition, in some parts of Britain there is a custom of boiling green vegetables in sodium bicarbonate to conserve the colour. The bicarbonate tends to destroy vitamins such as folic acid. Dr K M Laurence of the Department of Paediatric Research at the Welsh National School of Medicine, Cardiff, has speculated that in his part of the world (one of the regions where spina bifida is more than usually prevalent) this traditional practice may well contribute significantly to folate deficiency.

The possible (some would say undoubted) deficiencies we have discussed so far all relate either to obvious economic or social deprivation (as in many old people) or to particular practices that turn the currents of healthy eating awry (such as inappropriate traditional diets, or boiling in bicarbonate). The assumption is that if the simple ground rules of good eating, as outlined in the opening of this chapter, were pursued, then all difficulties would be resolved. However, there are a few cases that are not covered quite so neatly by the present canon, and on which the jury should remain in session.

For one thing, I have argued throughout this book and believe it in general to be so, that although we should not look naïvely to our hunter-gatherer ancestors for detailed instruction on how we should be eating, that we can at least gather the ground rules from them. And in general, I submit, this case stands up. High fibre, modest protein intake, low fat, variety – the characteristics of the 'natural' diet correspond neatly with modern recommendations.

Dairy food, however, does not fit as comfortably into the scenario as one might like. On the face of it, dairy food is 'unnatural': it is most peculiar for adult animals of one species to feed on the infant food of another. And, of course, there is plenty of reason for suggesting that the present emphasis on dairy food, both in modern agriculture and in the nutritional theories of the 1950s and '60s, is untoward: the secretions of cows contain more saturated fat than is good for us and more protein than we need. However, it has been pointed out, not least by Dr Roger Whitehead of the Dunn Nutrition Laboratory, Cambridge, that one vitamin in particular, riboflavin, can in practice be difficult to obtain in adequate amounts without recourse to dairy products. Of course riboflavin does occur in other foods, for example in liver (again) and in green vegetables. But he points out that in some African villages chronic riboflavin deficiency is common, and that in practice it would be difficult to correct without dairy products. Chronic riboflavin deficiency does not seem to matter greatly; cracked lips seems to be the only conspicuous effect. Nevertheless, the idea that people might actually *need* milk, in some small measure, is at least intriguing.

Of more widespread significance, perhaps, is the contribution of dairy products to daily calcium. It may yet prove to be the case (as outlined in Chapter 9) that marginal calcium deficiency may predispose to hypertension. It is certainly the case (though the matter is far from simple) that women in particular can be hard-pressed to sustain the calcium content of their bones, particularly when they bear children. Little old ladies are little partly for this reason, and archaeological remains, for example from Nubia at the time of the Pharoahs, show female skeletons markedly demineralised long before their owners would have qualified as 'old'.

Something needs to be done about dairy produce. Europe and the United States do have too many cows. Too much resource is spent on feeding them. The cows themselves suffer from the burdens placed upon them and that too, in a civilised society, is a serious matter. The fat they turn out is excessive. Yet dairy produce clearly has a place in feeding human beings, both in affluent societies and in poor ones. It's biologically odd that it should be so, but it seems to be so, nonetheless.

Then there is the possibility – it's only a possibility but it's an interesting one – that there may be even more to vitamin deficiency than has so far met most eyes. In Chapter 4 we briefly discussed Dr David Horribin's suggestion that many, if not most, human beings are chronically deprived of some essential fatty acids, notably gammalinolenic acid, alias GLA. GLA, says Dr Horrobin, might properly be regarded as a vitamin. Lack of it, he suggests, predisposes to many diseases, not the least being coronary heart disease. He may be wrong, but an idea as potentially significant as this (and which is based on several intriguing lines of evidence) does not deserve to be brushed aside. The fact is that diseases such as coronary heart disease are common, and no-one doubts that they probably have some basis in diet; and the idea that the dietary shortcomings may involve some micronutrient is far from implausible.

Finally, there is a school of thought which maintains that megadoses of vitamins, or at least doses many times the recommended intake, are a good thing. This school resorts, commonly and consistently, to various combinations of vitamin pills. Is this reasonable?

The sensible, conventional answer is no: a good, varied diet provides all the micronutrients you need, and evidence justifying excesses is lacking. Here again, however, a few additional comments seem in order.

The first is that gross excesses of some vitamins can be positively dangerous. In general, the dangers are generally held to be mainly confined to the fat-soluble vitamins A and D, which are stored in the body; and there were cases, for example, notably in the years after World War II, of unborn babies being damaged by their mothers taking huge excesses of cod liver oil, with its massive content of vitamin D, instead of the standard spoonfuls that were recommended. However, the dangers of excess are clearly not confined to A and D, and there is at least one recorded case of a fetus being damaged through its mother taking an enormous excess of folic acid in tablet form. This case was isolated and anomalous, but the fact that it occurred is one reason why the Medical Research Council felt that caution should be applied before folic acid supplements were widely recommended to pregnant women.

However, there is little reason to suppose that large doses of most vitamins are likely to be dangerous. Admittedly, some have pointed out that very large doses of vitamin C are a waste of time anyway since the tissues quickly become saturated and the excess is rapidly excreted through the kidneys. Others, however, have suggested that the tissues *should* be maintained constantly at saturation point in vitamin C, because vitamin C is an effective anti-oxidant and helps to protect the polyunsaturated fats in the cell membranes from degradation. One consequence of this, some maintain, is that constant saturation with vitamin C may help to reduce the risk of cancer. Again, the issue is unresolved, although it's clear, in general, that uncalled-for oxidation of delicate molecules in the body is one of the outstanding problems of all creatures living in the Earth's present atmosphere, which is rich in oxygen. It's clear too that ascorbic acid is one of nature's outstanding anti-oxidants, and clear as well that to maintain high levels in the body requires a constant high intake precisely because the body so readily excretes the vitamin. I will not presume to comment. But it may be that nutritionists will, as time goes on, recommend intakes of vitamin C that are far higher than at present.

There is also the point, extremely likely in the case of folic acid, and at least plausible in the case of GLA, that some people at some time in our society are vulnerable to arcane vitamin deficiencies of which we know little. The generalisation that we do not know enough to be complacent must be valid. It does not follow, however, that there is any particular point in stoking up daily on vitamin pills. Not the least of the many possible objections to such a course is that present-day multi-vitamins often do not include those that may be of critical importance. Few, for example, contain either of the two that we have singled out for discussion, folic acid or GLA.

It is no part of the intention of this book to tell you what to think. Expert committees who have looked carefully at vitamin deficiency in Britain have generally concluded that a good varied diet of fresh foods should leave you with no serious or even discernible vitamin deficiencies; and that view seems eminently sane.

The only caveats, which I believe are real caveats, are threefold. First, it is easier to slip below ideal intakes than you might suppose, as witnessed by the possible deficiencies of folic acid that could be exacerbated by cooking vegetables in bicarbonate solution. Secondly, that recommended intakes, though easily sufficient to prevent deficiency disease, may be below what is theoretically optimal, a possibility exemplified by vitamin C. And thirdly, vitamins may yet hold surprises, as suggested by Dr Horrobin's observations on GLA. None of these caveats adds up to a recommendation to take vitamin pills (unless recommended by a doctor for specific purposes), not least because arbitrary dosing with proprietary multi-vitamins has at best a kind of shot-gun feel about it. What it does mean, however, is that the whole arena of vitamins and minerals remains one of the most fertile for research. The spaces where these issues are discussed deserve to be watched.

Chapter 9

SALT UNDER PRESSURE

As people in western societies – or indeed in most societies – grow older, their blood pressure rises. The higher the blood pressure becomes, the more the individual is at risk from either of the two of the affluent world's commonest and most lethal disorders: coronary heart disease and stroke (the condition in which a blood vessel bursts in the brain). High blood pressure is only one of three outstanding risk factors for heart disease (the other two are smoking and high blood cholesterol). But for practical purposes it is the only outstanding cause of stroke.

Some doctors would argue that the rise in blood pressure with age is 'normal'. After all, it happens to virtually everybody, and it seems perverse to suggest that all of us are abnormal. If it is normal, then there isn't a great deal we can do about it – except what we do now. And what we do now is to identify those people whose blood pressure has risen faster and further than the rest, and label them 'hypertensive'; and then give them drugs to bring their blood pressure down. Usually, they must go on taking these throughout the rest of their lives.

This may be the only way. Hypertensives are not, for the most part, a distinct group of diseased people. True, a small minority do have an underlying disease, generally kidney disease, which is the cause of their hypertension. But most hypertensives are simply those people at the top end of the scale, who stand out from the crowd in the same way that a six-foot-six basketball player stands out from the common herd. The only difference is that being hypertensive is intrinsically dangerous – 'pathological' – whereas being six-foot-six is not.

However, many doctors, and indeed most people in general, subscribe to the belief – or faith, perhaps – that unhealthy conditions cannot simply result from failures of design. Being tall is not unhealthy, so we are happy to accept it as normal and do not seek to put a stop to the condition. But having high blood pressure is unhealthy, and we cannot accept that this is the inevitable fate of mankind. It must, we think, have a cause that we can do something about.

But hypertension, as we have seen, is a matter of degree. We all of us move in the direction of hypertensiveness as we age, and when everybody suffers from the same complaint it's hard to identify any one thing that might trigger it off. There are very few obvious correlations within our society that give a clue to cause. True, obese people tend to have higher blood pressure than people of average weight, and their blood pressure does go down if they lose weight. But obesity cannot be the cause of the universal rise that in some people culminates in hypertension.

What does cause hypertension?

Throughout this century there have been two outstanding candidates for the cause of hypertension. The first is psychological stress; and the second is sodium in the diet, most obviously in the form of sodium chloride, alias common salt.

On an individual level, psychological factors must play a part. Drive round Hyde Park Corner and your blood pressure will go up; and some people live every hour as if they were driving around Hyde Park Corner. Learn to relax (and relaxation can be learned) and your blood pressure will go down, at least in the short term. Learning to relax must be one of the most beneficial things that any human being can learn. The mistake, however, is to get carried away: to imagine that one clue amounts to a universal explanation, or that the one factor identified is the only factor. That such thinking is mistaken is obvious, but the fact is that some doctors who have very properly emphasised the influence of stress have at the same time sought to deny that any other factor could be important. That is simply foolish. All pathological conditions are multifactorial, and with conditions such as hypertension, in which the underlying physiology is immensely complicated (and far from understood), it is not only unsurprising but extremely likely that more than one factor is involved.

The idea that a high intake of sodium is a cause of hypertension was first proposed in 1904 – remarkably early when you consider that blood pressure could not be easily and routinely measured until the advent of the inflatable cuff at the beginning of this century. By the 1920s, the idea was well known. Then, in 1948, an American physician called Kempner devised a diet for reducing hypertension, which consisted almost exclusively of rice and fruit. The diet worked, at least in many patients.

Taken by itself, of course, the success of Kempner's diet proves precisely nothing. It is low in sodium, but it is also low in a great many other things, including fat; and it is high in certain components, notably fibre and potassium. Even if it was the lack of sodium that was doing the trick, this would not prove that excess sodium caused the condition in the first place. In any case, Kempner's diet did not work with everybody – even among those stalwarts who were able to stick religiously to a regimen of such monumental tediousness. But although there are scientists who like, for some reason, to suppress all embryonic ideas (with shouts of 'no proof!'), it is now widely acknowledged that when the problem is knotty, all leads should be followed up. The success of Kempner's diet at a time when most treatments for hypertension were completely ineffectual was remarkable, even if limited; and the idea that low sodium was an important reason for its success, was certainly too intriguing to abandon.

However, remarkably few people were impressed. Among those who were was Lewis K Dahl, from New York. Dahl was primarily a physiologist and so interested not exclusively in curing illnesses, but in finding out how the body works. He set out to discover, in an orderly fashion, whether there were indeed environmental factors that influenced blood pressure and, if so, whether dietary sodium was one of them. He chose to work not with human beings, which are extraordinarily difficult creatures to work with, but with rats.

The blood pressure of rats, under normal circumstances, does not rise with age. But Dahl found he could cause it to rise, in various ways. Outstanding among those ways was to give the animals a diet high in sodium.

Rats are not human beings. Nevertheless, as I have already said, the simple fact is that the reason we know a great deal about the human body is because scientists do experiments on other animals, which they could not do on humans. Literal extrapolation to humans of everything observed in animals is ridiculous; but it is equally ridiculous to suppose that animal experiments cannot be instructive. And the more one looks at Dahl's experiments, the more they seem to accord with what is observed in the human species.

The outstanding point was that the rats' response to dietary sodium was far from simple and was highly variable. Thus, when the rats were give a diet high in sodium, their blood pressure did not rise immediately. There was always a latent period.

In addition, different rats responded to a different extent. In some the blood pressure rose quickly and dramatically, and the rats soon died. In others the response was less marked. A minority hardly responded at all to the sodium in their diet. Their blood pressure remained inexorably low.

This observation is more remarkable than you might suppose. Laboratory rats are highly inbred. They are supposed, indeed, to be genetically uniform so that the experimenter can tell that whatever effects his treatments have are the result of his treatment and are not influenced by genetic variation. Yet these supposedly uniform rats showed an enormous difference in their innate response to salt. Human beings are not genetically uniform; indeed, the human species is among the most genetically variable of all mammalian species. If it is the case that human blood pressure responds to sodium intake in the same way as the laboratory rats', then we might assume that the blood pressure of human beings, exposed to the same large amount of sodium, would vary enormously. Such variation is, of course, what we do see among the population at large.

Dahl did in fact prove that the rats differed in response to sodium for genetic reasons. Indeed he bred the animals that responded most to sodium, and those that responded least, and produced two quite separate strains: the sensitive (S) strain, who responded to sodium; and the resistant (R) animals, who did not. He also showed that rats differed in the way in which they responded to withdrawal of sodium after their blood pressure had been raised. With some – after a latent period – blood pressure went down when sodium was reduced. With others, it remained high. Again, there are intriguing echoes in human therapy. When some hypertensive patients are put on a very low sodium diet, their blood pressure goes down; with others, it stays high.

Overall, then, we do not see sodium immediately pushing up every animal's blood pressure as soon as it is introduced into the diet, or immediately causing it to fall when withdrawn. We might imagine that blood pressure is regulated by a mechanism comparable to the thermostat in a central heating system – and a somewhat unpredictable thermostat at that. Sodium influences the setting of that thermostat: if it's introduced, then the thermostat may, after a time, be set higher. If it's withdrawn, then the regulator, after a time, may set at a lower level. But although the response to sodium was both unpredictable and variable, Dahl showed, after trials on 30,000 animals over several decades until his death in 1974, that overall it could be highly influential.

So much for animal studies. Evidence for the role of salt in causing hypertension in humans comes largely from epidemiology. Thus Professor Lot Page of Tufts University in Boston, Massachusetts, has collected data on blood pressure from all around the world. He has listed about 20 societies in which blood pressure remains resolutely low and even falls with age, instead of rising, as is so inexorably the case in our own society. The hypertension-free societies are almost as varied, genetically, as human beings can be: they include Chinese and

Australian aborigines, Greenland Eskimos, and various tribes of Africans. Furthermore, each of these favoured groups has close genetic relatives elsewhere in the world whose blood pressure clearly can rise in different circumstances. Indeed, among the blacks of the United States, who genetically have much in common with the blacks of present-day Africa, hypertension is especially marked. If it was not their genes that was saving all those peoples from hypertension, then it had to be environment. So what did these peoples' ways of life have in common?

In general, the answer was simple: they were all stone-age cultures. That, however, is supremely unhelpful because stone-age cultures are as rich and varied in their way as modern cultures. However, various scientists at various times have measured just about everything that can be measured among these favoured peoples. And when all those measurements were fed into a computer, one factor, in Professor Page's words, 'came roaring out of the statistics'. That factor was diet: and among the various dietary factors, the one that showed the strongest correlation with blood pressure was intake of salt. The comparison worked even at the minute level. Thus, in the Solomon Islands there are many societies with different ways of life. Some cook their food in sea-water and their blood pressure rises with age. Some cook only in fresh water and their blood pressure is low.

We have no definitive information, showing unequivocally that salt is the cause, or even the main cause, of rising blood pressure in our society, and therefore the main cause of the extreme high blood pressure known as hypertension. But we do have intriguing clinical evidence, beginning with Kempner, and many physicians have now tried putting hypertensive patients on a low sodium diet and have shown that it is effective for many people. We have Dahl's animal experiments showing that if sodium is the cause, and if humans do indeed respond in the same way as rats, then we could expect to see precisely the pattern of hypertension in human societies that we do in fact see. And we have the anthropological data showing that those societies that eat a lot of salt invariably show a pattern of rising blood pressure, and those who virtually do without salt are never hypertensive unless they have some particular underlying disease, such as kidney disease. In addition we now have as it were the *coup de grâce* – increasing evidence that the cell membranes of people with high blood pressure handle sodium somewhat differently, as it were less adeptly, than those of people with low blood pressure. We do not yet have an overall detailed picture of how sodium works its evil ways: but there now seems little reason to doubt that the mechanism will, not too distantly, be revealed.

Snags in the hypothesis

In general, then, and very properly it seems, more and more nutritionists are suggesting that we should all cut down on salt. This is not easy to do – processed food is often drenched in it, and professional cooks add it as a matter of course. Indeed as much as 80% of the salt we eat is derived from processed foods. But we can at least, all of us, stop adding it to our own cooking, or serving it up in the universal cruet.

There is, however, a snag. Or rather, there are two. The first seems, at first sight, to knock the entire sodium hypothesis sideways. In fact it does not, as we will see; but it must be mentioned. The second, though less dramatic, is altogether more intriguing and suggests that cutting down on sodium may be only the beginning of the trek. The necessary goal, it seems, is to establish a correct and delicate balance between sodium and other metals in the body, notably (it seems at the time of writing) calcium and potassium. Nutritionists in future years may be making more subtle recommendations, involving juggling acts with all three.

Let's look first at the evidence that seems to invalidate the sodium theory altogether. There is one difficulty, in the whole sodium story, that has always been worrisome. The hypothesis is that too much sodium leads to high blood pressure. It's clear that within any one society some people have higher blood pressure than others. It seems to follow – doesn't it? – that in any one society the people who have the highest blood pressure should be the ones who eat the most sodium.

Some studies, over the years, have shown that this is indeed the case – and some have not. Among those that have was one published in 1981 in *The Lancet* (Vol. I, p. 1097) by Dr Ronald Finn and his colleagues from the Royal Liverpool Hospital and the University of Liverpool. They assessed people's salt intake by a questionnaire, asking subjects whether they would add salt to particular dishes, namely meat, fish, eggs, salads, potatoes and vegetables. For each 'yes', they scored one point; so those who applied salt to everything had a score of six, and those who did not add it at all scored zero, and so on. The questionnaire showed that those who scored the highest did indeed have the highest blood pressure: and the results were highly significant statistically.

Outstanding among the studies that show no such correlation is one published recently in *Science* (1984, Vol. 224, p. 1392) by David A McCarron and his colleagues from the Oregon Hypertension Program. This study is based on the National Center for Health Statistics' Health and Nutrition Examination Survey, mercifully abbreviated to HANES I. HANES I supplied information on 10,372 individuals, who were deliberately selected to be representative of the US population as a whole. It showed the blood pressure of those individuals, and it showed their intake of no fewer than 17 different nutrients.

Analysis of the HANES 1 data showed not only that there was no correlation between sodium intake and blood pressure, but that there was actually a *negative* correlation. In other words, the people who consumed most sodium were the ones with the *lowest* blood pressure: and those who ate least sodium had the *highest* blood pressure. You could argue, of course, that the people with the highest blood pressure – the hypertensives – had already cut down their sodium intake and so confused the results: by such means are statistics sometimes confounded. But Professor McCarron and his colleagues were ready for that one. They deliberately excluded known hypertensives from the study, and only people who knew their blood pressure was high would go out of their way to cut out salt.

The HANES data are solid. The study was well conducted. The results, on the face of it, are very awkward indeed for what was beginning to look like a good, sound explanation of a dangerous human condition. Some have tried to suggest that there are flaws in the study and that there is no case to answer. But there are flaws in all nutrition studies, and such objections are usually foolish.

The fact is, however, that this study (and others that have failed simply to show a correlation between salt intake and blood pressure within a population) is nothing like so damning as it seems. Consider just two points. The first, as we noted in Chapter 6, is that there is no easy, straightforward correlation between food intake and obesity. It simply is not true that fat people, in any one society, consistently eat more than thin people in the same society. Yet no-one would doubt (indeed it would be absurd to doubt; it would be contrary to the most fundamental laws of physics) that surplus energy stores, in the form of fat, represent an intake of energy that is surplus – for the needs of any one individual. In short, even when we know that one environmental factor (in this case calorie intake) is the cause of a particular condition (obesity) we still do not necessarily find the correlation *within* any one population that some purists demand.

The second point relates to quantity. It's long been believed that human beings need a high intake of sodium. This belief has many roots, some of which are mythological. But it is also observed that salt is excreted in the sweat, and when people sweat a lot, they can lose a great deal of sodium. If that sodium is not replaced, then distress may result, including muscular cramps. Thus coalminers in Britain traditionally added salt to their beer, and soldiers in Kitchener's army were put on a charge if they failed to eat up their salt tablets.

The fact seems to be, however, that human beings need very little salt, perhaps in the region of 200 milligrams a day. They do indeed lose salt in the sweat, but this should be seen as a way of getting rid of the surplus. They do feel symptoms of deprivation in the short term if suddenly robbed of sodium – but only, it seems, because they have adjusted to a very high input and so suffer what, by analogy, might be seen as withdrawal symptoms. When people are given time to adjust to a low sodium intake they do not lose much in their sweat (indeed they sweat almost pure water) and do not suffer from withdrawal. Soldiers in the modern Israeli army, who spend their days under the desert sun, do not take salt tablets; and what they do not take in, they do not excrete.

But in western societies, sodium intakes tend to be at least 10 times what is physiologically required. In HANES 1, intakes varied from below 1600 mg to more than 5000 mg (that is, five grams). Everyone, then, in the study (which can reasonably be taken to mean virtually everybody in the United States) is on a very high sodium diet compared to what they need, and compared to the intake of aboriginal people whose blood pressure does not rise with age. If everyone is taking 10 times as much as they need, we would not expect to see a simple correlation between the amount of sodium ingested and the blood pressure. We may draw an analogy with lung cancer. Few now doubt that cigarettes are the prime cause of lung cancer. If you compare a million people who do not smoke at all, with a million who smoke 20 a day, then you will find that the latter will have significantly more lung cancer. But if everyone in the society was smoking at least 60 cigarettes a day, then the clear-cut association between habit and disease would be lost. Sixty cigarettes a day is so bad that it would be hard to show that 65 a day was even worse.

Such arguments explain well enough why you should not necessarily expect to be able to correlate blood pressure with sodium intake. But they do not explain why it is that HANES 1 showed a *negative* correlation – why those taking in least sodium were the most hypertensive. The reason could well be contained in the other minerals examined by the study. The people with the lowest blood pressure were those with the highest intake of potassium and the highest intake of calcium, and vice versa. A low intake of potassium or calcium (particularly of calcium) was likely to mean high blood pressure.

These findings are not surprising. It's been noted before that a proper intake of potassium and calcium is necessary to keep blood pressure down. To some extent, it seems, this finding may be directly related to the observation that – HANES 1 aside – a low intake of sodium is a good thing. For example, sodium and potassium have to be maintained in the correct ratio if the cell membranes are to function properly, and if sodium is raised then this ratio is upset – possibly to be restored by raising potassium.

Now consider the fact that in practice in the American diet, sodium and calcium tend to be associated one with another. For example, the principal source of calcium is dairy produce, including cheese, which of course commonly has a high sodium content. It seems very likely, then, that in the HANES I study the low intake of sodium is significant not because it is by any reasonable standards low (indeed it is at least 10 times more than is physiologically necessary) but because it is associated with a low intake of calcium; indeed the low sodium readings act as a *marker* of low calcium. And whereas sodium intake in the US is extremely high (by physiological standards), intake of calcium is probably hardly better than marginal. In short, the deficiencies of calcium and potassium shown in the HANES I study are probably real – people really are likely to have a marginal intake of these minerals; but the variations in sodium are entirely spurious, because the intake of sodium invariably is many times above what is necessary.

In short, the general idea that a high intake of sodium is a bad thing seems to be reasonably well established. Cutting down late in middle age may not contribute much to the well-being of any one individual (once the 'thermostat' is set, it may not be easily re-set), but helping to establish a fashion for low-salt diets, so that the next generation, for whom there is still hope, do not acquire a taste for it, seems eminently worthwhile. And salt is, undoubtedly, an acquired taste: people who have never been exposed to a salty diet do not necessarily take immediately to it and people who (like myself) give it up quickly find that gastronomic pleasure does not end because of it. There are plenty of ways to flavour food, including a cornucopia of spices, without salt.

However, the stories of potassium and calcium and, perhaps, of other minerals as well have yet to be properly worked out. Potassium should not be a problem. Vegetables, in general, are a good source, and all dietary recommendations in this book point to eating more vegetables. Vegetables and fruit (and even hard water) can also meet calcium needs though calcium is a potential problem especially for children, pregnant women and old people. Dairy food is indeed a principal source of calcium, and the more you cut down on milk and cheese to avoid saturated fat, the closer you could sail to a marginal intake of calcium. However, the fat in dairy products, which is the worrying component, is not rich in calcium: double cream is not a good source and butter is poor. The advice to cut down on milk fats, then, as opposed to the rest of that excellent product, remains unsullied.

The hypertension story, however, is far from concluded. Until there is a complete understanding of the mechanisms whereby blood pressure is regulated, and of the effects of minerals upon those mechanisms, and of the influence of diet upon those minerals, the discussions will continue. For those for whom watching nutritional theory unravel is something of a hobby, this remains an exciting area.

Chapter 10

THE SENSE OF STAYING SLIM

Anyone seeking to apply universal formulae to the problems of obesity, a single edict that would solve everyone's problems, is, as someone said of Winston Churchill during one of his more youthful escapades, either a fool or a mountebank. The reasons for obesity are complex, and different combinations of reasons apply in different people. There is no single definitive statement to be made about it, and no all-embracing formula to be applied. It is, however, possible to set out a few principles, and the first questions to ask are what is obesity, and is it a bad thing?

What is obesity?

Being obese means carrying too much fat. That raises two questions. The first is, how do you measure the amount of fat you're carrying? And the second is, how much is too much?

There are, nowadays, accurate ways of measuring the total fat content of the body. They involve, for example, measuring body potassium. But these kinds of measures are for specialist clinics or research units. For day-to-day purposes, including those of the average medical check-up, simpler options are called for.

The first is to pinch the flesh at various points (so-called 'skinfolds') and measure the thickness with callipers. This, in the hands of experienced people, is a useful guide of the ready-reckoner variety, but it clearly requires consistency and honesty and various other human qualities that are not easily guaranteed.

The second course is to weigh people. But people of the same sex and height may be all sorts of different weights, and they may be of different weights for all kinds of different, and legitimate, reasons. In particular, some are very muscular, and some have muscles, if detectable at all, like sash-cords.

At first sight, then, it seems that weight is a poor guide to obesity since fatness is only one of several reasons for being heavier than other people of the same sex and height. There are two saving clauses, however.

The first is that whereas differences in bone and muscle could well produce fairly modest differences in weight between people of the same height and sex, dramatic differences are far more likely to be due to differences in fat. Thus a perfectly fit, lean, weight-lifter of six foot may be around 12 stone, and a thin athlete of the same height, equally fit (in terms of his chances of living a long time), may be only 10 stone. This variation is only 20 per cent, yet it is between extremes of body types. Differences in fat content, however, can easily lead to 20 per cent differences. The 10-stone aesthete who lets himself go a bit may well reach 12 stones. And the 12-stone weight-lifter's identical twin brother, who prefers drinking to training, may rise to 18 stones – a 50 per cent difference between one individual and his otherwise identical sibling.

Secondly, beautifully trained six-foot athletes of 12 stone are a fairly rare breed. Most people of six foot who are 12 stone would, if they trained, be 11 stone, or even 10 stone-something. In short, by far the *commonest* reason for being heavy in our society is fatness. Fat causes the greatest variations in body weight and is the main cause of being overweight; and thus, in practice if not in theory, weight for height is a sound and reasonable measure of obesity.

Does obesity matter?

Insurance companies gear their policies to actuarial tables: lists of statistics that show as much as is measurable about human beings and correlate those measurements with mortality. And actuarial tables show that each person, for his or her height, has an ideal weight range within which their chances of survival are greatest (see chart opposite). If you are appreciably outside this 'ideal' range, then your chances of dying before your time are increased.

In practice, of course, many more people are significantly above their ideal weight than below it. After all, a person who was 50 per cent below his or her ideal body weight would be most unlikely to qualify for insurance at all: he or she would be emaciated, which in general means seriously ill. But many people are 50 per cent above their ideal weight. There are plenty of short 15-stoners around.

One reason that more people are significantly overweight than significantly underweight is that there is a very simple and natural way to become overweight: accumulating fat. As the actuarial tables show that significantly overweight people die earlier than people of ideal weight, then the question of whether it matters seems open and shut. Heaviness is a bad thing. And since, as we have seen, heaviness generally implies obesity, then obesity is a bad thing. QED.

Nothing is ever quite so simple, however. Heart disease is the biggest

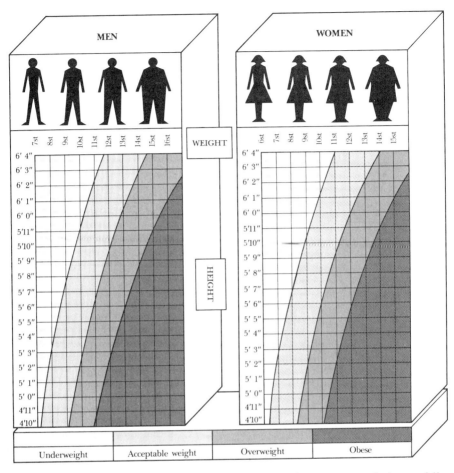

Figure 8 *Find the point where your height line and weight line meet to see whether you fall in the 'acceptable' weight range. (Figures charted by St Bartholomew's Hospital Medical Illustration Department, London.)*

single cause of death among men and, as we observed in Chapter 5, obesity has not emerged as an *independent* risk factor for heart disease; or, at least, the independent contribution of obesity *per se* is only small. That means if you are 50 and fat then you are more likely to have hypertension (which is a risk factor) and to have high blood cholesterol (another risk factor). But if you are 50 and fat and your blood pressure is low, your cholesterol is 'normal' and you do not smoke, then (some epidemiological studies have shown) your chances of heart attack are only slightly greater than those of a 50-year-old thinnie. In short, obesity is associated with risk factors but it is not *in itself*, apparently, particularly dangerous to the middle-aged man. It is merely associated to some extent with things which are dangerous.

This point is not entirely academic. Indeed it perhaps has not been taken seriously enough. After all, millions of people – men as well as women – spend millions of pounds trying to reduce their weight, and it's possible that they have chose the wrong target. Perhaps, instead, they should adopt courses of action that would reduce their blood cholesterol, or their blood pressure. The point is academic to the extent that losing weight is liable to reduce blood pressure anyway and could help to reduce blood cholesterol; but although it is likely to do the former, it need not do the latter. There are diets which *will* reduce blood cholesterol markedly, notably the very high fibre diets applied by Dr Anderson in Kentucky to diabetic patients (see Chapter 6), but although such diets may produce weight loss, they are not 'slimming' diets, and the lowering of cholesterol is not correlated with the loss of weight.

It is a little too glib, however, to suggest that obesity itself is not dangerous unless linked to some other risk factor. For one thing, heart disease is not the only issue. Extreme obesity has several undesirable consequences all its own: for example, it complicates surgery, should you ever need it, and may complicate childbirth. It is also something that people in general do not like and so detracts from enjoyment of life. More to the point, the statement that obesity does not greatly increase the risk of heart disease unless linked to one of the major risk factors is true only for middle-aged men. Young men between the ages of, say, 15 and 34 who are overweight but otherwise fit (fit enough, that is, to qualify for insurance without loading), do have a higher mortality rate 20 to 25 years later than men of the same age of normal weight. Fat young people, it seems, are more likely to fall foul of the major risk factors in later life. The fat middle-aged men who had no additional risk factors were (it seems) simply the lucky ones – those who escaped major risk factors despite being fat.

In short, being fat, in general, is a bad thing. And being fat, for practical purposes, means being appreciably above what the actuarial tables show is the ideal weight for your sex and height, where 'ideal weight' means the weight at which you are least likely to die. It's impossible to draw a sharp line between being slightly overweight, and being positively obese, and even being slightly overweight (given that the extra weight is likely to be due to fat) is not a good thing. But some nutritionists have suggested that obesity can properly be said to have begun in earnest when you are 20 per cent above your ideal weight. Twenty per cent may seem rather a lot. But even by that seemingly generous definition, obesity afflicts one fifth of western men and a third of western women.

So what can be done about it? There are dramatic ways of treating obesity. They include surgery (hacking away surplus fat, or by-passing reaches of the gut) or prolonged starvation, possibly abetted by drugs, or wiring of the teeth. These methods are for those few unfortunate people for whom obesity is a serious problem, sometimes even life-threatening, and practised only by medical specialists working from specialist clinics. These extreme cases are outside our brief. We are concerned here with the mass of humanity (no pun intended), for whom obesity is an inconvenience, with the unpleasant connotation that it may shorten life. We are concerned indeed with obesity not as an outright pathological condition, but as a state towards which many healthy animals, including human animals, will drift if surrounded, throughout life, by food and drink that is concentrated, attractive and easy to consume.

The principles of maintaining weight

It is very fortunate that everybody knows that getting fat is caused by eating too much food. It is very fortunate because if it was not so obvious, on a common-sense basis, then some scientists of the more pedantic kind would still be arguing the matter. After all, if it's true that an excess of calories leads to obesity then it ought (it seems) to be possible to show that fat people eat more than thin people. But studies do not show this, or at least, not consistently. Indeed they often show that fat people may eat less than thin people. There was a time when if a doctor put a person on a diet, and the person failed to lose weight, then the doctor would assume that the patient had been cheating, nipping off for a covert round of eclairs and angel cakes. Denial was no use: many a fatty has had charges of mendacity added to his or her misfortune.

In truth, clinicians often find, when they probe deeply, that their fat patients do consume more than they (the patients) think they do. Nevertheless, modern studies show that whereas some people are very good at burning off surplus energy, others are very good at storing it. People with an advanced capacity for burning energy may eat as much as 30 per cent more than people of the same age, height and sex with a propensity for storing it, and yet stay at the same weight. A 30 per cent difference is a very great deal. Thus, the average British man consumes around 2500 kcal a day. On 2200 kcal he would, as time goes on, lose weight. But there are people of 20 stone, who in this affluent environment must be considered unfortunate, who do not lose weight even on such a relatively modest intake.

But for any one individual there is no future of such niceties. If you are putting on weight, then it's because you are plying your body with more calories than it requires, or is able to dispose of by generating heat. The fact that you may think you are eating less than your pet canary has nothing to do with the case. In the matter of determining the relationship between food intake and fat stored, each human body makes its own rules.

But in the end, whatever ground rules your body lays down for you; whether you are made to be prodigal with energy or to cleave to surplus calories, you are subject to the laws of thermodynamics: the relationship between work and energy. Food supplies you with energy, which is measured in calories (or rather, as a calorie is too small a unit, in kilocalories – kcal). You expend those calories in two ways. The first is in general metabolism. This includes staying warm – which is not, incidentally, a large consideration for big animals such as adult humans, though it is for smaller ones and may well be for un-clad babies – and day-to-day running and repairs, including energy for the transport of materials in and out of body cells. The second is in activity (getting out of bed, cleaning the teeth, running the London Marathon). If you consume more calories than your body can dispose of, then it stores the surplus as fat – 9 kcal per gram of fat. In practice, it tidies the globules of fat away in special tissue known as adipose tissue: and because adipose tissue contains things other than pure fat (notably water), adipose tissue provides about 7.5 kcal per gram.

Clearly, you will stay slim (let us say, at your ideal weight) only if the amount of calories taken in equals the amount expended: so far, at least, we are dealing in simple Micawberish economics. Thus, in principle, there are three ways in which you can reduce weight, or avoid putting it on. These are:

1   Reduce intake of energy.
2   Increase rate of metabolism.
3   Increase activity – that is, exercise.

The first point, perhaps, is that the body, unbidden by us, is remarkably good at adjusting its weight. Consider, for example, a hypothetical but very typical young man of five foot eight inches who at the age of 20 weighs 10 stone: a slight figure, but by no means skinny. At 30 this same young man might weigh 10 stone 10. At 40, he is 11½ stone. At 50, having 'slowed up a bit', and after many a business lunch, he weighs in at 12½ stone. He still is not fat, though even his friends now agree that he is stocky, going on portly.

This man, we will assume (as would be typical), has spent very little time worrying about his weight, or consciously slimming, and has exercised only for the fun of it. And it shows, you may say: after all, his weight has increased 25 per cent over 30 years. The slim young man, without undue gourmandising, has become the tubby middle-aged gent.

But consider what this 25 per cent means. For two decades he put on only one pound a year. That's just 1¼ ounces a month – about 35 grams: too little to register on the bathroom scales.

Let's look now at our hypothetical man's food intake. As a fairly typical western man, he takes in around 2500 kcal a day: about 75,000 a month. The 35 grams that he puts on in a month represents a store, in the form of adipose tissue, of around 265 kcal. Thus, if we assume that his body 'wants' to maintain a constant weight, we see that it is inaccurate to the tune of 265 kcal in every 75,000. That's an inaccuracy of about one part in 280: to be precise, 0.35 per cent. Considering the variety of food and drink our hypothetical but typical man puts down his throat, and the erratic nature of its delivery – sometimes great excesses, sometimes modest privation, such accuracy is astonishing.

In truth, though the above argument has been widely promulgated, and does have a pleasing logic to it, we need not credit the human body with quite the precision that is suggested. For one thing, energy that is surplus to immediate requirements is not converted into fat with perfect efficiency. A gram of stored fat will indeed supply 9 kcal. But the act of converting ingested food into stored fat itself consumes a certain amount of energy; so you need to take in more than 9 kcal in order to store 9 kcal-worth of fat. This means that the body has a little more leeway than at first sight seems to be the case.

In addition, we have said that a person of 11 stone may not require more food than a person of the same height who is only 10 stone, because the two may differ in the extent to which they store or jettison surplus calories. But if any one person increases his or her weight from 10 stone to 11 stone, then he or she will require more food to stay at 11 stone. Thus if our hypothetical man ate the same amount all through his life, then he would sooner or later reach a weight at which his requirement did indeed match his intake. If he wanted to progress from slim young man to tubby middle-aged gent he would have to keep raising his intake, so that it was always slightly ahead of his requirement.

The point remains, however, that even if your intake of energy is only slightly surplus to your requirement, then, over a few years, and certainly over a few decades, the increase in weight can be spectacular. The body may indeed be very good at adjusting its own weight. But very small percentage discrepancies, over time, have an enormous cumulative effect.

Yet people tend to think about obesity only when, one day, it strikes them, or they are told, that they are getting fat. They then, typically, seek some dramatic reversal of that state; and indeed, in western countries, spend hundreds of millions of pounds sterling a year to that end. Yet the key to the whole business is not the dramatic assault on past indulgence, but constantly and continuously to tip the balance ever so slightly in favour of the mechanisms that try so hard, despite our worst efforts, to keep us in trim. Avoiding obesity, for most people, should not be a matter of 'slimming'. It should mean, simply, avoiding that surplus of a few hundred calories a month (storage of less than 10 kcal a day in the form of fat) which, over a few decades, means 30 lb or so in weight.

Principle and practice

All this is all very well (and indeed undeniable) in principle, but it is not quite as easy as it seems. It is certainly easy to reduce energy intake by 300 kcal a month: that is the equivalent of a couple of standard British pork sausages. No great sacrifice. It's easy, too, voluntarily to increase energy expenditure by a few hundred kcal a month: a few brisk strolls would do that. It seems, then, on the face of it, that anyone could stay the same weight just by eating very slightly less, or adding the occasional stroll to their pattern of exercise.

The joker in the pack, however, is metabolic rate. Your energy intake is under your own direct control. So, too, is the amount of exercise you do. But what really counts is your overall metabolism, which is not under your direct control. Changes in metabolic rate may spoil the best-laid plans.

For instance, it's obvious that if you eat more than you expend then the surplus may wind up as fat. But it is not obvious that if you eat 100 kcal more than you seem to need (plus the bit required to put the energy into store), that you will necessarily accumulate 100 kcal-worth of fat. Your body might simply step up the metabolic rate in response and save you from your own indulgence. On the other hand, if you reduce your food intake by 100 kcal per day, you will not necessarily lose weight either – or at least, not commensurately with the deficit. Your body may slow its metabolism, ever so minutely, and so save the 100.

The same kinds of ideas apply in principle to attempts to burn off surplus energy by exercise – though here matters seem to be in our favour. Thus exercise may expend disappointingly little energy: a shattering game of squash is worth only a few hundred calories. But there is evidence that exercise raises metabolic rate, and the 'afterglow' continues to burn off at least some energy after the game itself; although, in truth, such 'afterglow' is far greater after very heavy exercise than after modest exercise.

Thus, on the one hand it's easy to be euphoric about losing weight (or maintaining weight) and point out that a daily energy deficit of just a few kcals will cause you inexorably to lose weight. But on the other hand it is equally easy to be totally despondent and point out that doing a little bit here and little bit there is of no use, because the metabolism will adjust and go its own sweet way, and you will be back where you started.

However, neither euphoria nor despondency are called for. It's certainly true that trivial concessions to losing weight, the odd pint of beer sacrificed or the odd block walked around now and again, will make very little difference. But it is quite obviously untrue that we have no control at all over our own weight. The art of losing weight is to arrange a daily energy deficit (using more energy than is ingested) and it is possible to do this, whatever adjustments the body may make. Furthermore, as we suggested above, the key to the whole process is slow but steady. Interludes of heroism are a waste of time. What's called for is to develop habits that will last a lifetime. Food is the subject of this chapter: energy intake. But first a word about voluntary expenditure. Trying to stay slim against a background of absolute slothfulness is, to use a rather apt metaphor, an uphill struggle.

The value of exercise

Doubting Thomases there are, quite a lot of them in fact, who will maintain that exercise, as a way of losing weight, is a waste of time. Some have pointed out that if you do more exercise you simply increase appetite; and others, that the amount of exercise done has to be enormous to make any significant difference. Both statements require severe modification; and, for practical purposes, are nonsense.

The relationship between appetite and exercise is one of those very difficult and unglamorous topics on which it is extremely hard to carry out good, statistically valid studies, and on which, consequently, hard evidence is thin on the ground. However, some common-sense statements are worth making. The first is that there is clearly both a short-term and a long-term relationship between energy used and food eaten. Thus in one study, soldiers on training sessions did not increase their food intake in the first week, but they did do so as time went on. Their appetite took time to catch up with their needs, but, in the end, it did catch up. In the longer term, it's clear that people doing hard physical labour every day, such as lumberjacks and coalminers, do generally eat considerably more than people in more sedentary jobs. It's also clear that exercise, in some forms, *can* give you an appetite. Therefore (some have argued) exercise is worthless because it just makes you eat more.

However, a little sober reflection shows that the relationship between exercise and appetite is by no means simple. Both the soldiers adjusting to exercise within a week or so, and the coalminers adjusting over a lifetime, are extreme cases. Both groups, in short, are fit. As George Orwell pointed out in the 1930s (though the comment does not seem to be quite so true today) you never see a fat coalminer. With these examples we are seeing the body *in extremis*: the amount of physical work done in a day is far above usual limits, and the individual must eat his head off just to keep body and soul together. With the soldier on operations we indeed see the body as a machine, working flat out, to the limits of the energy than can be put into it.

It's true too, as I have said, that exercise can give you an appetite. But what do people mean by such a comment? Any runner will tell you that the last thing he feels like after a half-marathon is food. He's far too hot, for one thing, and it takes several hours to cool down enough to want to eat. No, what most people have in mind when they say that exercise promotes appetite is a stroll in the open air. However, the same amount of energy expended on a rowing machine in a hot gymnasium would not promote appetite to anything like the same extent. It's not the exercise that gets the gastric juices flowing, so much as the cold wind and the sense of anticipation.

On the other hand, there is evidence that a moderate amount of exercise helps to *adjust* appetite. At the other end of the scale from the paratrooper who eats huge amounts in order to do a day's work, is the unfortunate fatty who eats because he or she has nothing else to do: eating, indeed, becomes the only form of exercise. The psychology of this is too intricate to probe here; but there is some evidence that a simple lack of activity is one of the causes of the added intake of food.

In between the extremes (and the extremes do not really interest us much, as they are rare compared to the average) there is good evidence that most of us have a good idea, albeit an unconscious idea, of what we think is a reasonable amount to consume. If we took a job down the mines, we doubtless would adjust that preconception. But if we added a little bit of exercise to our daily rounds, there is no reason to suppose that we would commensurately increase our intake. We might even decrease the amount we consumed.

The second objection to exercise is that it can play little part in adjusting weight because you need to do an enormous amount of work to lose a small amount of weight. Thus a kilogram of fat (just over a couple of pounds: not enough to win a round of applause at weight-watchers) provides 7500 kcal. This amount would take you through the London Marathon, and the Boston, and the New York. Or, if you preferred, you could do it all in one go and run from London to, say, Dover.

On the face of it then, exercise is hopeless. But all that such statistics prove is that marathon-running is not a good way to lose weight. Let us consider the matter more soberly and return to the point that weight should be lost slowly and steadily: or that the way to avoid getting fat is to avoid the ounce-by-ounce accumulation. A marathon – 26 miles – is a long way. One mile is not too bad. One mile is worth about 100 kcal. One mile a day is 700 kcal a week. That's 36,500 in a year. That's equivalent to 4·85 kg of adipose tissue in a year – getting on for a stone. I am not suggesting that running a mile a day is particularly easy, or that if you do it, you will lose a stone in weight over a year. But it is the case that although simple arithmetic shows how foolish it is to use exercise as a way of losing large amounts of weight quickly, that same arithmetic reveals the theoretical value even of modest amounts of exercise, done regularly, in the long term.

In addition, as Geoffrey Cannon and Hetty Einzig point out in *Dieting Makes You Fat* (Century Publishing, 1983), exercise does have a knock-on effect. It does appear to raise metabolic rate for some time afterwards, which is a bonus; and it also tends to convert fat into muscle tissue, which has a higher metabolic rate than fat tissue.

In short, common sense suggests that regular exercise ought, other things being equal, to help you to lose and maintain weight. And common sense, in this as in most things, should not be lightly put aside.

This brings us at last to the other determinant of weight that is under voluntary control: energy intake.

Intake of energy

Fasting, under medical control, has a place in the treatment of extreme obesity. But for most people it is ridiculous; and so, too, is the 'crash diet'. Statistics show that enormous amounts of weight lost quickly are soon put back on again.

One reason why weight lost in crash diets is quickly restored is that crash diets, in general, are extremely tedious. Only people with an iron will can keep to them, and those with iron wills perhaps do not commonly get fat in the first place. Another reason is that the weight loss from crash diets is highly deceptive.

The body stores energy in the form of fat. But fat is a *long-term* store. In the short term – that is, for hour-by-hour purposes – the body stores energy in the form of glycogen, which is a polymer of glucose similar to starch. Glycogen provides far less energy than fat does: about 4 kcal per gram, or 4000 per kilogram, against the 9000 kcal provided per kilogram of fat. More to the point, adipose tissue contains remarkably little water – only about 15 per cent – so that a kilogram of adipose tissue provides 7500 kcal. But glycogen is accompanied by huge amounts of water; roughly, 25 per cent glycogen to 75 per cent water. Thus, glycogen·

(because it is effectively diluted) provides only about 1000 kcal per kilogram.

When you go on a crash diet, you first (in general) burn off the glycogen stores; those stores, after all, are more readily mobilised. At the same time, you jettison the water that accompanies that glycogen. In a day, if you completely starved yourself, you could run up an energy deficit of 2000 to 3000 kcal; and your weight could well fall by a kilogram or more. By the end of a week of near starvation, you could well have lost about 4 kg; and thus do people return from 'health farms' claiming to have lost 10 lb or more.

But most of that loss will be from the glycogen/water pool. Most of the loss, indeed, is water. As the diet continues, fat is mobilised to replenish the pool; and, broadly speaking, 1 kg of mobilised fat contains enough energy to restore 7·5 kg of glycogen/water. Indeed, as the semi-fast continues, weight loss may cease, or even temporarily be reversed.

If fasting continues, then of course the fat stores begin to dwindle. So too, incidentally, do the muscles, weight for weight, at about the same rate. Thus, a week of starvation could indeed produce a 'genuine' weight loss of around 3 kg, of which about half is fat, and half is muscle. Complete starvation is, of course, potentially highly dangerous. But the point we are arguing here is that the dramatic weight loss achieved by starvation, or by the semi-starvation of heroic dieting, is not sustained; or at least, it does not remain dramatic. As a long-term strategy, heroic dieting leaves a great deal to be desired.

We keep coming back to the idea of slow but sure. The maximum energy deficit you could engineer for yourself in a day would be about 7000 kcal: that would be the result of complete starvation combined (if such a thing were possible) with a day competing in the Tour de France. And although that 7000 kcal in the short term would produce dramatic weight loss, it in fact represents a loss of less than 1 kg of adipose tissue. Better by far to think of trying to arrange a deficit of, say, 500 kcal a day, which is 3500 kcal a week, which is equivalent to around 2 kg per month, which is a highly impressive, and genuine, 20–24 kg in a year, which is getting on for four stone.

Now put these comments about intake together with those concerning exercise. A marathon a day is ridiculous. Even a mile of running a day is a bit of an effort. But for long-term, permanent weight reduction, we should be thinking only in terms of arranging an energy deficit of a few hundred calories a day; and for maintaining weight, for preventing that inexorable rise, we're trying only to avoid that small and constant surplus that may be only a few tens of calories a day above what the metabolism can burn away. On this day-to-day scale of things even the traditional brisk walk, and certainly the bicycle instead of the 'bus, can make a significant contribution. So too, can tolerable, as opposed to heroic, changes in diet.

Eating to be slim

No 'diet' follows. The problem we're addressing is lifelong maintenance of weight close to the ideal. This will not be achieved by once-and-for-all heroic efforts, but by a lifetime of sensible habits: habits composed of several elements, of which reasonable exercise is one, and temperate food intake is another. The habits relating to food intake are of two kinds. The first concerns behaviour: and the second relates to the nature of the food itself.

In 1967 Dr R B Stuart published what proved to be a seminal paper in *Behaviour Research and Therapy* (Vol. 5, pp 357–365) entitled 'Behavioural Control of Overeating'. In the 1970s, scientists and clinicians at Stanford University in California developed his ideas into what proved to be a highly effective treatment for obesity. In the 1970s in California (as in much of the United States), obesity was – rife, I think the word is. And at Stanford Dr Joyce Nash and her colleagues showed that many people were fat largely because they paid no attention to eating. They never felt particularly hungry, and they never felt particularly full. They simply ate, off and on, more or less all day: hamburgers, milk-shakes, tuna fish on rye, fizzy drinks, whatever was going. Many of the most grossly obese people literally ate unconsciously; they were not aware that they were opening their mouths and putting things in.

That particular *modus vivendi* was undoubtedly more common in the US than in Britain; after all, the US is far more advanced in the art of 'fast food', which is designed to be eaten on the hoof. It also, presumably, was more of a problem in the 1970s than now: certainly obesity is no longer particularly conspicuous in California. Nevertheless, the Stanford observation is instructive – and so is the solution.

The solution Dr Nash devised was to restore the ritual to eating. She established ground rules: never eat without sitting down; always eat with a knife and fork; and so on. By such means people regained control over what they consumed; they were no longer sabotaged by their own unconscious habits.

The Stanford approach (like every other approach) is limited: it would not solve everybody's problems, or, probably any one person's problems completely. There are plenty of fat ladies (and gentlemen) who would not dream of eating anything without linen tablecloth, napkin and cruet. But the generalisation that underpins the study does have universal validity: don't eat without thinking about what you're doing; don't nibble just for comfort, whether it's sweets, or peanuts, or potato crisps. Take control, is the universal message. Taking control is the *sine qua non*.

The second approach to reducing calorie intake is, of course, to think about the nature of the food itself. The fortunate thing is that, to a large extent, the other recommendations in other chapters of this book cover most of the ground.

Thus in Chapter 5 I argued that it is useful to reduce fat intake. This by itself would not necessarily reduce your total intake of calories. But if you also follow the advice in Chapter 6, which is to derive the major proportion of your calories from unrefined carbohydrate – and particularly to avoid sugar – then you will almost certainly lose weight. After all, it is extremely easy to take in, say, 200 kcal by eating a high-fat food: Cheddar cheese is a high-fat food and a mere 50 grams – about two ounces – will provide 200 kcal. It's easy, too, to take in 200 kcal as sugar: half a litre of Coca-cola, which is about three quarters of a pint, will provide that amount. But to derive 200 kcal from unrefined carbohydrate can be fairly hard work. That's more than half a pound of boiled potatoes; about a pound of apples; half a pound of bananas; a quarter of a pound of boiled rice, or of wholemeal bread; a couple of pounds of carrots; and a veritable mountain – about five pounds – of boiled cabbage. To derive 3000 kcal per day from our standard western diet is easy – many a man does this with three comfortable meals. But 3000 kcal from boiled potatoes is around eight pounds: or, if you wanted to vary it, six pounds of potatoes and eight pounds of carrots.

Thus, from whatever standpoint we begin, whether it's a direct assault on heart disease or some other disease of affluence, or a simple attempt to lose weight for aesthetic or other purposes, we finish up with the same eminently commonsensical dietary advice: cut down on fat and eat carbohydrate only in unrefined form, which means regarding sugar only as a rare spice. The nice thing about modern nutritional theory is the way the different threads weave together.

QUICK QUIDE TO GOOD DIET

Energy comparisons

As we have already seen, the energy (or calorie) content of different kinds of foods varies enormously. Weight for weight, and mouthful by mouthful, fat has many more calories than unrefined carbohydrates such as cereals. So it is useful to have some comparisons to use in everyday life. Eating food rich in energy is more likely to result in an excess of calorie intake than eating bulky food, because the latter makes us feel full more quickly so we eat less of it.

Food Equivalents in Kilocalories

One pint of whole milk has 370 kilocalories which come from protein (17%), fat (55%) and carbohydrate (28%)

Approximately the same total calories come from:

FOOD	AMOUNT (grams)	PORTION (approx.)	PROTEIN	FAT (kilocalories provided in %)	CARBO-HYDRATE
Wholemeal bread	175	6 slices	16	12	72
Jacket potatoes	440	1 lb (400g)	10	1	89
Apples	1080	8 apples	2	0	98
Semi-sweet biscuits	83	12 biscuits	6	33	61
Digestive biscuits	80	5 biscuits	8	40	52
Cod (steamed/grilled)	400	1 lb (400g)	87	13	0
Roast lean beef	240	8 thin slices	74	26	0
Butter	50	2½ pats	0.2	99.8	0
Low-fat margarine	100	5 pats	0.2	99.8	0

Menu comparisons

These two menus highlight the differences between the average British diet and the NACNE recommendations. They both provide approximately 2800 kcal.

This day's menu has the typical dimensions of the average British diet in that just over 40% of the energy (calories) is derived from fat, of which a high percentage is saturated.

MENU A

Breakfast
Cornflakes with milk and sugar
2 slices wholemeal bread with
butter and marmalade
Tea or coffee with milk and sugar

Mid morning
Coffee with milk and
sugar, and biscuits

Lunch
Sausage or pie and chips
Tomato ketchup
1 pint of beer

Mid afternoon
Tea with milk and sugar, and a
cheese roll

Supper
Meat casserole
Mashed potatoes
Buttered peas
Fruit pie and cream
1 glass of wine

Bedtime
Coffee or tea with milk and sugar,
and biscuits

This menu conforms with the NACNE recommendations in that less than 30% of the energy (calories) is derived from fat, of which less than a third is saturated. It also has a lower sugar and far higher fibre content.

MENU B

Breakfast
Fruit juice
Wholegrain cereal with
semi-skimmed milk and sugar
2 slices wholemeal bread with
polyunsaturated margarine and
marmalade
Tea or coffee with semi-skimmed milk

Mid morning
Coffee with semi-skimmed milk

Lunch
2 rounds wholemeal ham
sandwiches
1 pint of beer

Mid afternoon
Tea with semi-skimmed milk
Fresh fruit

Supper
Grilled chicken or other lean meat
Jacket potato
with polyunsaturated
margarine
Sweetcorn
Runner beans
Fruit pie (with wholemeal pastry)
and yoghurt
1 glass of wine

Bedtime
Coffee or tea with semi-skimmed milk
Toast and polyunsaturated
margarine

Swap list

Jam/marmalade	try reduced-sugar jam/marmalade
Fruit stewed with sugar	try fruit stewed with sweetener
Canned fruit in syrup	try canned fruit in natural juice
Sweetened carbonated drinks	try low-calorie carbonated drinks or unsweetened fruit juice
Sugar, white or brown	try sweeteners (tablet or liquid form)
Sugary snacks	try fresh fruit or dried fruit
Sugar on cereals	try fresh fruit or dried fruit
Fruit yoghurts	try natural yoghurt with fresh fruit added
Confectionery	try fresh fruit or dried fruit or low-sugar products
Mixers	try low-calorie mixers
Roasted salted peanuts	try fresh peanuts or pieces of raw vegetable
Homogenised silver top milk	try fresh skimmed or semi-skimmed milk
Cream; evaporated or condensed milk	try natural low-fat yoghurt
Hard English cheese	try mature English cheese and use less or mature Continental cheese and use less or reduced-fat cheeses
Luncheon meat, salami	try lean ham or cold poultry
Paté	try cold meat
Fried meat	try grilled or roast meat
Fried fish	try grilled or poached fish
Roast sirloin	try roast topside
Shoulder of lamb	try leg of lamb (lean)

Butter/Margarine	try low-fat spreads
Chips	try very large chips or jacket potatoes
Unspecified vegetable oil	try oil high in polyunsaturated fat
Tinned fish in oil	try tinned fish in tomato sauce
Flaky and shortcrust pastry	try choux pastry
Salt in food	try herbs and spices to flavour
Salt at table	try using salt cellar with smaller holes